Open Horizons

The Fesler-Lampert *Minnesota Heritage Book* Series

This series is published with the generous assistance of the John K. and Elsie Lampert Fesler Fund and David R. and Elizabeth P. Fesler. Its mission is to republish significant out-of-print books that contribute to our understanding and appreciation of Minnesota and the Upper Midwest.

SIGURD F. OLSON

Open Horizons

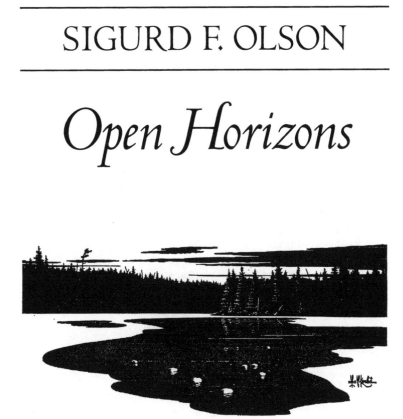

ILLUSTRATED BY LESLIE KOUBA

University of Minnesota Press

MINNEAPOLIS

First published in hardcover in the United States by
Alfred A. Knopf, Inc., New York, and simultaneously in Canada by
Random House of Canada Limited, Toronto.
First University of Minnesota Press edition, 1998.
Reprinted by arrangement with Robert K. Olson,
Yvonne O. Olson, and Sigurd T. Olson.

Portions of this book have appeared in *Audubon* and *The American West*.

Acknowledgment is hereby made for permission to quote from
"The Historical Roots of Our Ecological Crisis" by Dr. Lynn White Jr.,
as it appeared in *Science* (March 10, 1967), Vol. 155, pp. 1203-7.
Copyright 1967 by the American Association for the
Advancement of Science.

Published by the University of Minnesota Press
111 Third Avenue South, Suite 290
Minneapolis, MN 55401-2520
http://www.upress.umn.edu

Printed in the United States of America on acid-free paper

Library of Congress Cataloging-in-Publication Data
Olson, Sigurd F., 1899–1982
Open horizons / Sigurd F. Olson ; illustrated by Leslie Kouba. —
1st University of Minnesota ed.
p. cm. — (The Fesler-Lampert Minnesota heritage book series)
Originally published: 1st ed. New York : Knopf, 1969.
ISBN 978-0-8166-3037-0 (pbk. : alk. paper)
1. Natural history—North America. 2. Natural history—Outdoor
books I. Title. II. Series.
QH102.039 1998
508.7—dc21 98-21095

13 12 11 10 09 08   10 9 8 7 6 5 4 3

TO ALL VOYAGEURS

WHO HAVE GAZED INTO

OPEN HORIZONS

ACKNOWLEDGMENTS

I AM FOREVER GRATEFUL TO MY WIFE, ELIZABETH, FOR LOVE, constant faith, and wise counsel, and for understanding patience during the long years when I explored open horizons in many far places; to Ann Langen for skilled editing, sound judgment, and enthusiastic participation in the preparation of the manuscript; to Angus Cameron for invaluable suggestions as to planning and organization; and to Alfred A. Knopf, who conceived the basic idea of the book.

ACKNOWLEDGMENTS

Appreciation for permission to use excerpts from many books goes to A. F. Barnes Co., publisher of *The Poems of Henry Wadsworth Longfellow* and *Five Fur Traders of the Northwest*, edited by Charles M. Gates of the University of Minnesota Press; to Francis P. Harper, who edited *Alexander MacKenzie's Famous Voyages from Montreal 1789–1793, The Journals of Alexander Henry the Younger and of David Thompson 1799–1814*; to Charles Scribner's Sons for a passage from Henry Van Dyke's *Days Off*; to the University of Minnesota Press and the author for a quotation from Grace Lee Nute's *The Voyageur's Highway*; to G. P. Putnam's Sons for use of the last verse from "The Voyageur," in William Henry Drummond's *The Voyageur and Other Poems*; to Oxford University Press for statements from Aldo Leopold's *Sand County Almanac*; to Charles T. Brantford Co. for the comment of Yellowstone Kelly in *Lives of Game Animals* by Ernest Thompson Seton; to the University of Miami and the author for Juan Ramón Jiménez's essay "Arts and Democracy," Hispano-American Studies No. 2; to the Sierra Club and Wallace Stegner for an epigraph in *The Place No One Knew*, by Elliot Porter; to Harper and Row for quotations from Teilhard de Chardin's *The Phenomenon of Man*; to Crown Publishers for a statement from *Einstein's Ideas and Opinions*; and to E. P. Dutton for quotations from *Far Away and Long Ago*, by W. H. Hudson.

I am deeply indebted to Archibald MacLeish, Alberto Giacometti, Justice Felix Frankfurter, Harold Means, Ber-

ACKNOWLEDGMENTS

trand Russell, and others from whose lectures and writings I have gleaned ideas and quoted.

I am thankful to the following for inspiration and vision: Joseph Wood Krutch, Loren Eiseley, Lewis Mumford, Aldous Huxley, Julian Huxley, Le Compte du Nuoy, Owen Barfield, Harrison Brown, Boris Sokoloff, N. J. Berrill, and André Malraux.

CONTENTS

INTRODUCTION

IN TRAVELING GREAT RIVERS AND LAKES, THERE ARE TIMES WHEN islands fade, hills and headlands recede, the water merges with the sky in a distant mirage of shimmery blue. These are the open horizons of the far north.

If it is calm, the canoes drifting through reflections with nothing to break the vast silence but the hypnotic swish of paddles, there are moments when one seems suspended between heaven and earth. If it is stormy and the lake alive with whitecaps and blowing spume, each instant is full of battle and excitement. When, after hours and sometimes days, the misty outlines of the lake take form again, islands slowly emerge and float upon the surface, headlands become real, one passes through a door into the beyond itself and the mystery is no more.

Life is a series of open horizons, with one no sooner completed than another looms ahead. Some are traversed swiftly while others extend so far into the future one cannot predict their end. Penetrations into the unknown, all give meaning to what has gone before, and courage for what is to come. More than physical features, they are horizons of mind and spirit, and when one looks backward, we find they have blended into the whole panorama of our lives.

Those of childhood show the dawning awareness of beauty at a time when the Pipes of Pan can still be heard; those of youth retrace the ages of mythology, the long millennia of the hunter and the freedom of the wilderness. The open horizons of young manhood bring broader concepts, the impact of knowledge, reverence for the living world, relationships to others and to the earth itself; those of maturity, concern for the living-place of man, perspective on his long journey from the primitive, and understanding of the great imponderables that once filled his dreams.

What a man finally becomes, how he adjusts himself to his world, is a composite of all the horizons he has explored, for they have marked him and left indelible imprints on his attitude and convictions and given his life direction and meaning. What one remembers of any expedition are not the details of rapids, camps, or miles of travel, but rather a montage of major headlands passed, and the sweep of the land.

Open Horizons is the story of the unknowns I have discovered, and gone through. No two voyageurs enter their doors in the same way or have identical adventures, but all have in common the final impact which is in the evolution of vision and perspective, and when there are no longer any beckoning mirages ahead, a man dies. With an open horizon constantly before him, life can be an eternal challenge.

OPEN HORIZONS

In these prosaic days
  Of politics and trade,
Where seldom fancy lays
  Her touch on man or maid
  The sounds are fled that strayed
Along sweet streams that ran;
  Of song the worlds afraid;
Where are the Pipes of Pan?

OSCAR FAY ADAMS

CHAPTER I

THE PIPES
OF PAN

THE PIPES OF PAN SOUND EARLY BEFORE the sense of wonder is dulled, while the world is wet with dew and still fresh as the morning. To remember when those elfin notes were first heard is almost impossible, but this I believe is true, that long before recognition, the music has been heard. The look of wide-eyed delight in the eyes of a child is proof enough of its presence.

My first recollection came one sunny afternoon when Mother led me through a grove of maples in the fall. That day the trees must have been in full color, for the ground was deep in drifting leaves. As we walked through them we were surrounded with color, and when the wind blew we were drenched with it. The swirling masses of red and yellow filled me with excitement, and when we ran through the grove, ran and ran until we could run no more and sank laughing to the ground, color and beauty became part of my life. So vivid is the memory, I can still hear the rustling of the leaves in my dreams and see the wild, free bursts of exploding color.

Once at Fort Churchill on the coast of Hudson Bay, some sixty-odd years from that first experience, I found myself again part of swirling color. It was September and midnight and the northern lights were playing as they can only in the far north. I walked down the main street of the little town and the lights were suddenly all around, whirling, enveloping, carrying me with them. Again the sense of being part of moving, living color, of being covered and immersed in it; and while time had changed me, the Pipes sounded then as clearly as those of long ago.

I heard their music in many places as a child, but one of the best was an alder thicket where I used to hide, a veritable jungle that had never been cleared. The swamp began just beyond the garden fence and I went there often, burrowing my way through the maze into its very center. There I had fashioned a nest on a dry little shelf. It was cozy and warm, and like any hidden creature I lay there listening and watching. Rabbit runways ran through it and birds sang in the branches around me. Around the edge was a fringe of tall grasses, but the ground itself was cushioned with sphagnum moss, and little pools lay around me like jewels. During

THE PIPES OF PAN

the summer, even at midday it was dark under the alders. In the fall when the grasses were sere and the sun shone, those pools were flecked with blue and gold.

Sometimes a great snowshoe rabbit hopped along one of the trails, and often I saw mice with beady eyes and trembling ears. No great thoughts, revelations, or new wisdom came to me, but something happened that I did not realize until long afterward. I became part of all the beauty, the tiny sounds, and everything around me.

The alder swamp was my refuge and no one came there but me. Only Mother knew, and she understood it was mine and mine alone. What I heard there were the Pipes, and what I sensed, I know now, was the result of a million years of listening and being aware, the accumulated experience of the race itself and of ages when man was more a part of his ancient environment than now.

Not long ago my grandson Derek disappeared while we were at my cabin on Listening Point. Not greatly concerned, remembering my own childish needs, I searched just the same and finally found him sitting on a rock near the shore of the lake looking down into the water. Though he had heard me, he did not move or look up.

"What are you doing?" I asked finally.

"Just sitting," he said, which was perhaps as good an answer as anyone could give.

I left then and did not disturb him again, for he was listening to the Pipes. The rock was a place of wonder and delight just as the alder swamp had been to me, and as time went on his mind would be filled with things he had sensed, many more than he would ever be able to recount or re-member. Some would stand out more boldly than the rest, and I wondered which they would be, but even as I questioned him, I knew there was no answer, for out of his vast complex of impressions time would do the sifting.

My first trout fishing is as vivid today as it was one summer morning when I hiked across a green meadow with an older boy heading for a little creek which wound through the sedges. On the way we caught grasshoppers for bait, putting them in a box, where they scratched and rustled and whirred their wings. I had never seen a brook trout, *fontinalis*, and this was the beginning of a lifetime love affair which has never dimmed.

"Be quiet," cautioned my partner. "If you make any noise, you'll scare them."

We barely breathed as we stalked the creek, finally stopped at a place where it made a sharp bend. We could not see the water, for the grass stood tall along the banks, but we heard it, a soft gurgling just beyond.

My rod was a slender tamarack wand, peeled carefully and weathered a golden brown with the knots shaved close to the stem, the tip as resilient and tough as bamboo, the line a length of black sewing thread, the hook bought for a penny at the store. It was bronze in color, its point sharp as a thorn. I baited it, pushed the pole over the grass, the hopper kicking its long legs, fluttering its wings, twisting and trying to fly. A pert brown marsh wren lit in a bush overhead, twittering excitedly.

I lowered the grasshopper toward the water, moved it

6

up and down, felt it touch the pool; the tip of the rod bent sharply and there was a splash as a trout took it. With a heave I lifted the fish out of the water and threw it far behind me on the ground, turned and threw myself upon it. To me that first trout, shining and glittering in the sunlight, was a creature of unbelievable beauty. The back and sides were mottled with olive and black, spotted with dots of burning red, the belly white and silver and pink along the edges. The fish twitched and quivered as I held it in my hands and I could feel its icy coldness.

My creel was bedded down with cowslips growing close to the water, and as I laid my prize on the crisp, green leaves, I stood there gloating and happy. Then we moved to another pool, and so it went until the basket was full and heavy and it was time to go home.

That day made a trout fisherman of me, and I have never lost my love for the little speckles of back-country creeks. Once I said that trout fishing is a spiritual thing, and after a lifetime, I know it is true. For that matter, all fishing is a spiritual thing to a boy, no matter what he catches. The sense of surprise, the eternal wonder of a fish coming out of the water, the deep inherent sense of primitive accomplishment in getting food by simple means, and the Pipes always playing softly in the background—no wonder all boys love fishing, no wonder all men, who are really boys at heart, feel the same.

Below my home was another creek flowing under a log bridge. Why it was called Jump Creek I do not know, but it was probably named during the logging days when some lumberjack was forced to jump across it to escape the logs plunging down from the sluice above.

Under that bridge lived rock bass, and I often ran down there in the morning before going to school. Lying on a log beside the water I looked down into the amber depths of a dark and gloomy place. At first I could see nothing, but as my vision cleared, the cavern became golden with light. I lowered my hook with its pink squirming angleworm just far enough so it could be seen by the bass. The worm wriggled and stretched its long free end, winding back upon itself and around the end of the line until it seemed hopelessly entangled, then working itself free once more.

No hunter knew more of a thrill than I lying there watching and waiting. Had my quarry been a monster fish in some tidal river or a mastodon along the forefront of the glacial ice during its retreat from northern Europe, my suspense could not have been greater.

Then like a shadow, a bass moved out of the dark into the golden light below me, hung there, its tail fanning slowly, fins moving in rhythm, gills opening and closing. Imperceptibly the fish moved closer to the bait, its round eyes rimmed with red, its mouth open wide. In an instant the worm was swallowed. A jerk on the line and the bass was hooked, dashed back toward its hiding place, only to be brought out of the water to my grass-lined creel. I never caught more than two or three, but though I went there a thousand times, the thrill and wonder of it never left me.

Those early years were full of fishing. Even in my dreams the creeks and rivers of spring haunted me, the sound of running water, oozing rivulets from suddenly warmed banks, dogwood stems flaming in the sun, the birches of the ridges turning purple in their tops. Arbutus were always blooming on southern slopes, pussy willows swelling over the snow, yellow cowslips brightening the edges of swamps. Then the smells, the bittersweet resins of Balm of Gilead, masses of balsam in the first real warmth, the thawing earth itself, a combination of odors so powerful it was as though the air were surcharged with them. All this colored my days, for this was the awakening and the beginning of life after the long sleep of winter. At times it seemed I too must burst with the swelling buds, grow as they grew, reach for the sun, run over the hills along the streams and through the woods giving vent to the joy and excitement within me.

One night in April I dreamed of catching two large white fish in a river several miles from home. The vision was very clear and there was no doubt of where to go. As soon as my morning chores were done, I headed for the river and went to the very spot of my dream. The stream was swollen with the first rains and the melting, and its water murky from the reddish clay along its banks. Alder, dogwood, and willow stood knee-deep in the flood.

I found an open place, tossed out my line, let the worm drift deeply below me. Almost immediately a fish took hold, a large one by its weight; it was all I could do to hold it against the current. Finally tiring, it came flopping to the surface, a great white one, as I knew it would be, a sucker of about three pounds, unbelievably large and beautifully silvered, its belly brushed with pink. Carefully, I slipped a cord

9

through its gills and mouth and tied it to an alder bush nearby.

No sooner had my worm begun to sink than I had another exactly like the first, and with two on the stringer, their combined weight bent the alder branch dangerously. For an hour I tried for a third, but there were only two, and when I gave up at last, I was happy as only a boy can be when he's been fishing in the spring.

It may have been happenstance, but it could also have been a recurrence of the intuitive sense all primitives and children seem to possess, a knowing beyond intelligence, reason, or instinct, a blending of thoughts and hopes, a reaching down into the deep pools of racial memory, a feat modern man seldom knows because of what he has lost through the welter of impressions that have bombarded his senses from the time he was born. Children fortunate enough to have lived in the woods or the open country during their first impressionable years often have it, but even they lose it swiftly and only on rare occasions does it return.

Usually this early sensitivity is so completely covered over with the calluses and scars of civilization and a multiplicity of sensations hitherto unknown that by maturity it is lost forever. Tribes relatively untouched by modern man still have it, the strange power of sensing and seeing into the unknown, of understanding without being told, of knowing what cannot be seen. This ability, which we call clairvoyance, is looked at with suspicion and distrust, for those having it are different from the rest.

It is not surprising that a boy living as I did should dream of fishing in the spring. The importance to me is that the dream came true, and as a result long years afterward I trusted dreams and intuitions. They did not always materialize, but some of them did.

Once on an expedition in the far north I was confronted with a difficult choice, for the river we had been ascending divided into two similar streams. Our maps did not show the fork, so if my choice were wrong it would mean many miles of hard travel up a swift and dangerous waterway full of sharp rocks, treacherous rapids and falls, with days of precious time lost. I sat at the juncture wondering what to do when suddenly the decision came to me, and without hesitation I took the branch to the left. Deep within me I knew the course I had chosen was right.

Another time when I had lost a boy on a canoe trip through wild country and no amount of searching or trailing seemed to do any good, the same thing happened. The youngster would starve if we did not find him, and in the trackless waste where he had disappeared his body might never be found. I remember vividly the end of the long search when everyone had given up hope how I sat on a windfall wondering what to do. I had covered the country for miles around, crossed and recrossed it time and again, trying to figure out what the boy might have done in his wanderings. I prayed then, long and silently, poured out my hopes and fears in a final desperate attempt to find a solution. Somehow in the process I must have aligned myself with forces, thoughts, and feelings beyond understanding, dipping once again into that great unplumbed pool of darkness involved with the spiritual background of all mankind.

I shall never forget the calm that came over me, a sense

of resignation and acceptance of a power beyond me that somehow I had touched. I rose and started off through the woods, following a route as unerringly as though it were blazed. Within three miles over bogs and rugged hills, I found the boy sitting on the bank of a beaver flowage he had crossed, and when I saw him, I was not surprised. I looked at him for a long time, and the Pipes were playing softly as they always do when a man has listened to their music and followed it to its source.

The other evening I paddled out with Derek to catch a bass for supper. The loons were calling and the boy was using a light rod as a special concession. It was dusk, the witching hour, and the west was stained with sunset, a time of magic when anything could happen.

The canoe drifted near a log, just close enough for a cast at a circle of ripples from a rising fish.

"Now," I whispered.

The fly settled gently near the swirl and the bass was on, a good one of possibly a pound or a pound and a half, just big enough for supper. A dash for the log, then out of the water dancing on its tail, and a final dash under the canoe before I reached with the net and brought it in.

The Pipes were plain that night, and I know Derek heard them as I did, though mine perhaps were a muted obbligato to the strains of old.

Not all of my early adventures had to do with fish and fishing. They had to do with mice and squirrels and birds, all the creatures around me, and though I soon learned to hunt and kill, strangely enough it did not seem a violation of my inherent love of all living things. Within me still was the feeling of primitive hunters for their quarry, an empathy born of untold millennia of intimate involvements and dependencies on other creatures for survival.

Hunting rabbits in the fall after they had turned white and before the coming of the snow seared my memory, and even today when I see a startling flash of white in brown autumn woods, my heart misses a beat and I am transfixed with wonder.

An old friend of the family owned a beagle hound, and long before I could handle a gun he took me with him hunting, sensing that we had something in common. A tall gangling sort of a mountain man, there was about him an air that set him apart, a sense of awareness perhaps, that in later years I was quick to recognize in others, a belonging and easy familiarity with woods or mountains, but above all to a boy there was a friendliness and companionship that transcended all other considerations.

To this day I can hear the beautiful sound of the beagle's baying, and remember the listening as the dog followed the age-old circle of its prey, the excitement in its notes as the rabbit neared, the high quivering tremolo of all Bugle Anns on a hot trail. In that music I could read the progress of the chase, the almost unbearable suspense as the animal neared —then a white ghost floating through the brown underbrush, no haste in spite of the closeness of its pursuer—the roar of the shotgun, and a violently kicking form on the leaves.

To those who do not know, this may sound as though a blood lust was mine, but this was not true. Mine was a natural reaction, part of an ancient need, and the music of the Pipes sounded clearly through it all.

There were other times too, times that had nothing to do with fishing or hunting, when they played as gaily. One of them was when we were snowbound and it was impossible to go to school. The snows seemed deeper then, for there were no snowplows or buses. Children walked to school except on rare occasions when some farmer would come around with a sleigh to take us through the drifts if they were not too deep for the horses. To awake some morning to find snow so heavy there wasn't a chance of anyone getting through meant joy and ecstasy. Though there were many such times, I remember one of the very first, when Father went to the door after breakfast, looked out into the swirling whiteness, then put on his greatcoat, scarf, and mittens.

We watched excitedly through frosted windows as he shoveled a path to the barn three or four feet deep, with the snow still coming down. It seemed he was gone a long time, but there was a horse to feed, the chickens, a dog, and some tame rabbits. At last he returned, stomped off the snow, and came inside. We waited breathlessly.

"I don't believe the horses can make it," he said. "Snow's too deep even now. A big team might, so there's a chance."

We accepted the possibility and got ready for the long, cold ride, sat bundled up for an hour, but no horses came, no creak of great runners, no shouts out of the whiteness. There were no telephones, no television or radio, no way of getting word. School would be closed for days when the roads drifted over.

The snow kept falling, and through the ice ferns covering the windows we watched happily until there was only a blur outside. The drifts soon reached the window sills and the path Father had shoveled was level once more.

We could go nowhere, isolated as though on a desert island, our sense of removal complete. Why a child should have gloried in that situation is not hard to explain, going back, no doubt, to a time when forebears were removed by storms and floods and the innumerable physical limitations of a primitive existence from doing anything or having to conform to the wishes of others. There was food and water, shelter and warmth. Father and Mother may have worried, but for us our trust was complete and we knew only security and protection. The blizzard could last a week or a month for all we cared, and in our hearts we hoped it might go on forever.

My brothers and I built a fort at one end of the room, and when we tired of that played chess and checkers, and at last settled down with our favorite books. It was a time of joy that I have never forgotten. The Pipes played softly all the time and our hearts were full. There was nothing to disturb the quiet, nothing of moment or pressure, no distracting tensions, influences, or problems. No adult can ever know such sustained contentment, but there are moments that do come all through life if they can be recognized, moments that hark far back to the first dawning awareness of what removal actually means.

Years later on a rocky, windbound point in the far north I caught the sensation again. We had fought our way all day from island to island, dodging behind any protection we could find, hugging the lee shores in our canoes, braving the wild open stretches, avoiding wherever possible dangerous open sweeps. In spite of the gale we had made progress and it looked as though we would reach our goal by nightfall. Ahead lay a long promontory, bare and sinister in full sweep of the wind. Paddling desperately to reach it, icy spray whipping over us, we dared not go beyond its point whatever lay ahead, so we landed in its lee, climbed to the top of the ridge and leaned against the gale.

Enormous waves crashed against the black rocks, and as far as we could see were miles of whitecaps, long rows of waves, the far shore shrouded with mist. Canoes could not live out there. In that frigid clime if we overturned or swamped or lay awash, it would mean death.

We returned to the canoes, paddled down the shore until we found a place where we could land safely. On a level spot out of the wind we pitched our tents, anchored them firmly and made ourselves comfortable, dried our food, sleeping bags and personal gear, and did all the many things postponed because of constant travel. Pinned down and stormbound, we were stranded with no possibility of going anywhere until the wind abated.

I climbed again to the top of the sheltering ridge above us and watched the combers march across the bay. I had the old feeling of detachment and removal from the world of struggling mankind, schedules, logistics, problems and solutions, and man's ravishing of his environment. Here was the old wilderness where nothing had changed, and should civilization come, it would come here last of all.

Someone called and the spell was gone, but for a moment the Pipes had sounded above the crashing of the waves and a sense of the old phantasy of long ago was mine. While I stood there I was one with all adventurers, all explorers, and those who had ever looked into the unknown, part of a forgotten world of glory and romance, where things cannot be seen unless there is belief.

A story is told of Arthur Conan Doyle sitting in his garden with a little boy who did not believe in fairies.

"There are fairies here," he said, "and if you watch close you might see them."

The boy was skeptical as Sir Arthur told him where to look. It was dusk and the time had come. For a while they saw nothing and the boy became impatient and restless.

Suddenly Sir Arthur said, "There's one," and he pointed to a low hanging bush in the far corner of the hedge.

"Right close to the ground. I can see him plainly."

The boy looked intently. "I see it," he whispered, "exactly where you told me to look. I see the fairy."

Faith and belief had brought that fairy out as it always does, faith that they really exist, and belief in the spirit world. This world of trolls, fairies, and pixies is alive among primitive people everywhere as it is in all children for a time. Only when reason dispels phantasy do they disappear. They still dance to the Pipes of Pan and those who hear can see them.

Children live in a world not only of their own, but peopled with all they imagine. Their lives are rich and colored because of it, just as those of adults are enriched by their knowledge of all that has gone before. But the young have a special faculty of listening and understanding and are conscious of the unseen. During my early years I instinctively sought out places where the feelings were strong. One place I came to know long after the days of the nest in the alder swamp was a great pine near the shore of a lake. I used to curl up there on a bed of pine needles between two roots; I was part of the pine and the pine of me, for I could feel it move in the wind.

Sometimes a squirrel would come down to the lower branches and watch me with wide-eyed excitement. I listened to its chatter, to the nasal tones of the nuthatches, and the moaning of the wind in high branches.

Many years later when I read how W. H. Hudson felt when he went out in the moonlight to the acacia trees, I knew this feeling was not mine alone.

"I used to steal out of the house," he said, "when the moon was at its full, to stand silent and motionless near some group of large trees, gazing at the dusky green foliage silvered by the beams; and at such times the sense of mystery would grow until a sensation of delight would change to fear and the fear increase until it was no longer to be bourne and I would hastily escape to recover the sense of reality and safety indoors where there was light and company. Yet on the very next night I would go there again.

"The sensation experienced on those moonlight nights among the trees was similar to the feeling a person would have if visited by a supernatural being. . . . This faculty of instinct of the dawning mind undoubtedly is the root of all nature worship from fetishism to the highest pantheistic development. . . . Anthropologists go to the ends of the earth to seek for its survival among savage tribes. . . . Wordsworth's pantheism is a subtlised animism, but there are moments when his feeling is like that of a child or savage when he is convinced that the flower enjoys the air it breathes."

Such vivid awareness is swiftly lost today, but if it can be held into adulthood it enriches and colors all we do. How often in the wild country of the north I have been aware of the spirits of the voyageurs, the shadowy forms that once roamed the rivers and lakes. Often at night it seemed I could hear ghostly songs coming across the water, the rhythmic dip of paddles and the swish of great canoes as they went by.

Pipes of Pan, the little people, the spirits of trees, of animals and birds, of rocks and waters, of sun, wind, and storm, of night and morning, of a world all but forgotten in the hard, cold light of the technological civilization we have built; these were part of my early childhood, a time before reason and knowledge colored perception, days that not only were mine, but belonged to the childhood of the race.

The Pipes no longer sound as often or as clearly as they once did, but I know they are there and that children still hear them. I can tell by the light in their eyes, the sudden catch in their voices, by the constant listening and awareness of things that may be lost to me. I know that in the Pipes and their music and in the faculty to comprehend lies the difference between man and all other forms of life. He can understand and imagine, can reflect upon himself and the universe with a perspective no other creature possesses. Man alone has a vision of the past and the future and a consciousness of beauty and meaning.

*A boy's will is the wind's will
And the thoughts of youth are long long thoughts.*

HENRY WADSWORTH LONGFELLOW

CHAPTER II

THE WIND'S WILL

THE DAYS OF WIDE-EYED WONDER MERGED
gradually into a new era of growing physical activity and exploration of the countryside. Awe and surprise were still there, but now it was coupled with a hunger for new experiences that could not be denied. I ran the woods savoring everything, indulging my senses, absorbing smells, sights, and sounds as a sponge absorbs water.

The adventures of Daniel Boone, Kit Carson, Natty Bumppo, and all the romantic figures of the frontier peopled my dreams. I seldom visited the alder swamp or the great pine any more. Before me now was an open horizon with un-limited vistas and a life full of action and excitement. Henry Ware, the hero of the Altscheler books, and Cooper's Deer-slayer were the epitome of all the wild, free characters of the past. Because of them I knew the Ohio Valley, the Wyandots, Hurons, and Iroquois, as well as the dark and bloody ground of Kentucky.

Long before I could carry a gun, I used to hike into the brush near home. Following old logging roads and deer trails, I gradually extended my roamings for several miles into the back country. Though it had been logged and burned long before I came, this to me was the great unknown, as beautiful and untouched as the settlers first found it. Clearings were rare and few others went there. The land was grown with young aspen, birch, and balsam, a few relic pines, and clumps of hemlock from the old stands of virgin timber. Scattered everywhere were thickets of hazel, alder, and striped maples, jungles that intrigued me almost more than the big trees themselves.

Close to a tiny spring-fed creek I built a shelter of boughs and lined the inside with fragrant tips of balsam. The brook gurgled and sang as it tumbled out of a pocket of huge hemlocks that had escaped the logging and the fires. Behind me was a great rock sheltering my camp from wind and rain. From a short distance no one could tell that this was my home, for it looked like an old windfall nestling against the rough gray surface of the ledge.

In front I built a fireplace hedged with stones and over it placed a stick for my blackened cooking pot. The food I

ate was either roasted over the coals or boiled, birds and
squirrels killed with a slingshot, rabbits I snared, crayfish,
clams, or fish from the creek. With a pinch of salt and a bit
of bread such wild food tasted better than anything brought
with me. My first meal there was a whiskey jack, one of the
gray Canadian jays who found me at once. There were three
of them, their soft, ventriloquial warbling all around. When
one was almost within reach, I took careful aim with my
slingshot and brought it down. Bigger than a robin, I was
amazed how small it was when stripped of feathers. I roasted
it over the fire and all but ate the bones. One day I found
several clams in a muddy bend of the creek, opened their
glistening, iridescent shells, and boiled them in the pot. Those
shells became my plates and I used them also to keep food
warm on the coals, marveling always at their beauty in the
light.

Once as I sat in my small refuge I heard a sharp crack.
I waited breathlessly as another stick snapped closer than
before, and a deer stalked out of the balsams, following a
trail I had used. The animal came very near, its big eyes
liquid and brown, its ears moving constantly. At the creek it
stopped, drank daintily, and picked its way carefully through
the shallows not more than twenty feet away. It must have
caught my scent then, for it stopped, head held high, blowing
air sharply through its nostrils. With a bound it cleared the
bank and vanished.

At that moment I was one with the Deerslayer and with
all the old hunters I had heard about. These men killed only
for food, fought bear, wolves, and mountain lions, lived off

the land and scorned the softness of settlements. In my wilderness camp I dreamed their dreams and saw the woods as they did. One of the old settlers living near seemed to understand my feelings and one fall took me to his little bush farm some fifteen miles from home and far beyond the area of my explorations.

On an eventful November day before the first snowfall, he let me go out alone with his 30–30 Winchester.

"Follow the deer trail," he said, "walk slow and listen, and when you come to a side hill, find a place where you can look over the valley. Stay quiet there and wait. When you shoot, I'll come."

He handed me two shiny shells, showed me how to load, and left me. The rifle was big and heavy, but that day it had no weight, and as I followed the trail I moved with my heroes. White snowshoe rabbits scampered off before me, but I was after bigger game. I walked slowly, stopped often to look and listen, and when I got to the side hill, found a big pine stump from which I could look down into the valley. I stood on its broad, flat top for hours, or so it seemed, but there was no cracking of the brush, not a flash of a white tail, not a sound to disturb the autumn stillness. A rifle cracked far in the distance, but nothing came my way. Toward late afternoon, I climbed down from my stand and hiked back to the cabin. Old John was loading our gear into the buckboard, for this was our last day and we must be on the main road before dark.

"Put the rifle under the bag of oats," he said, "where it won't move."

I ejected the two shells, saw that the gun was put away safely, then climbed up on the seat beside him. Old John clucked to the horses and we started down the road. The west was red, the air full of the smells of down leaves and dampness. I said nothing and he sensed my disappointment and was sad with me.

"Don't feel bad," he said, as we jogged down the narrow tote road. "The time will come, maybe next year. You are young, someday you will be a deer hunter."

The sky grew redder and redder, for there were forest fires over the horizon and smoke lay heavy to the west. A year is such a long time to a boy! If I could only see one, I knew I could bring it down! The buckboard jolted and swayed along the brush-bordered trail, and sometimes partridge whirred up from their feeding to light in the tops of the aspen. I watched them without interest as they sat unconcerned picking off the buds, thinking only of the deer I might have gotten that afternoon.

The horses clattered around a sharp turn and there in plain sight, not fifty feet away, stood an enormous buck with wide spreading antlers. Old John stopped the horses and we did not move.

"The gun," he whispered. "Slow; the deer will stand."

The gun—the gun, where was it? It should have been beside me, and to my horror I remembered how carefully I had placed it under the sack of oats in the wagon box.

"Under the oats," I breathed, "under the sack behind us."

"Careful," he warned. "Slow—no noise; I'll hold the team."

I slid back of the seat, rolled the heavy bag to one side, pulled the gun free, slid it out of its case.

The great buck stood silhouetted against the red sky; I could have hit it with a stone. The horses tossed their heads and the reins slapped. Old John handed me the two shells and I trembled as I slipped them into the magazine, opened the breech, and with a click sent one into the chamber. At the sound, the buck stiffened, looked toward us, and as I struggled to my feet, went off the road in one enormous bound. A telltale flash of white and it was gone into the rosy dark.

Old John said nothing, clucked to the horses, and we moved on. I sat beside him crushed and heartbroken, my big chance gone, the most beautiful buck in the world. What a triumph it would have been; I was sure life could never be the same again, never another hunting season. Disconsolately I ejected the shells, slid the rifle into its case, and looked straight ahead.

Again my old friend tried to console me. "You are young," he said. "There will be more times."

He was right, but that lost first chance burned so deeply into my boyish soul I have never forgotten. The Pipes sounded softly that night, but their music was doleful and sad. Looking back to that disappointment, I know now that it was part of growing up, for all hunting was not joy, there were hardships and frustrations as well, and being a good woodsman and hunter meant taking the bad times with the good.

Then came the red-letter day when I acquired a rifle of

my own, a .22-caliber single-shot Stevens. I had saved a long time for it, and when I finally had $3.87, I went to the post office, bought a money order, and sent it off. After what seemed like weeks, the long box arrived and I unpacked it with excitement and trembling. The blueing was unscarred, the stock shiny and dark. I oiled it carefully, polished it until it shone, and went back of the barn to fire it for the first time. Each day I practiced until by fall I could hit a mark no bigger than a silver dollar at fifty feet.

Partridge abounded in the aspen groves not far from home, and in the early mornings I hunted there almost every day before school. Those mornings were rich with the spicy smells of wet aspen leaves on the ground, the sounds of rustling everywhere, the colors of red and gold in the trees and over the earth. There were great, blackened stumps where once had been a forest of pine, and after the inevitable fires, aspen and birch had come in to heal the wounds and provide the cover partridge needed. Huge logs lay everywhere, good drumming places in the spring. I used to see those gorgeous males, bronze ruffs stiffly extended, tails spread like golden fans, strutting sedately from one end of a log to the other, finally to pause and beat their breasts in the rolling tattoo that could be heard for miles. All summer long I watched the growing broods from their first frightened flutterings to the time when they too strutted and exploded like bombs into the trees.

An old logging road wound through the aspen grove, grown with clover, its edges sand and gravel. Here was the best hunting of all, and as I walked quietly down its center, I looked ahead for the dark forms of birds that had come out to feed. The instant I saw one, I waited until the tense outstretched necks relaxed and the feeding began again, then slowly stalked my prey. It never occurred to me to shoot on the wing, as bullets were far too costly for that, so I crept forward until close enough for a shot through the head, sometimes twenty feet, but never over fifty. I could not afford to miss, and must not spoil the meat by a body shot.

Those heads with their black, beady eyes were never still. I would drop to one knee and aim when within range, holding my breath until I was absolutely sure. At times the sight would blur, and while I waited for my vision to clear, the birds often thundered off into the brush. Marking their flight, I would follow through the noisy leaves, listening for the slightest sound that might betray their presence. Usually a soft clucking warned me for they were always poised and ready for flight long before I saw them. When the moment came, I would aim once more and if lucky there would be a wild threshing on the ground.

These creatures were beautiful to me, their mottled brown and black, the cinnamon spread of their tails; I would kneel beside each bird, smoothing out the rumpled feathers. Mother must see them at their best, and I was never prouder than when I held them up for her admiring inspection. At the end of the season there were many hanging on the woodshed wall with the white snowshoe rabbits, food for the long winter ahead. I went there often to see the dappled sheen of their plumage in the sunlight, remembering where each had been taken.

Those first years of my Daniel Boone days had many facets, and though hunting and fishing played a major part, there were other experiences that influenced my thinking, molding early convictions of an entirely different kind. The dangers and hardships of the pioneer days were unknown to me, the starvation and suffering, the threat of Indian attack, torture when captured, the uncertainty and dread under which many lived. All I gleaned from avid reading and imagining was the exhilaration of adventure and the freedom they knew in roaming unsettled country. Even so, I knew intuitively how they felt, for their frontiers were also mine.

Not far from home was Star Lake, surrounded by virgin timber that for some reason had never been cut. The white pines stood tall and dark, just as they had all over Wisconsin before the harvest began. Many were over a hundred feet in height and three to six feet through at the butt. There was little underbrush and the ground was soft and deep with a carpet of golden needles. Great windfalls lay there, the ancient ones, the dead, and they too were covered with needles and mosses; small trees had taken root upon them, each a seedbed for the forest to come.

It was always twilight beneath those trees, for the tops met overhead, nuthatches sang far up in the sunlight, their nasal twang sounding everywhere, and squirrels chattered and scolded, busied themselves with burying cones in late summer and fall. I went there often to walk, or to lie for hours looking up through the high canopy above.

A creek ran through this magnificent grove, the water as dark as the shadows. No one bothered to catch such small fish as speckled trout, for there were larger fish in the lake itself. In the spring-fed stream the trout were never more than eight or ten inches in length, but their red spots flamed like rubies. All the times I fished there I never met a soul. The creek was shallow, but there were many little riffles, deep swirling holes under the banks and near the rocks, and whenever a log lay across it, trout were underneath. Their startling color excited me, but the great pines and the silence made them very special, far more than the fish themselves or the taking of them, something compounded of the environment of which they were a part.

In looking back, there was a growing appreciation of deeper meanings, and if there were no intimation of perspective, the primeval scene, its solitude and sense of removal, was becoming part of my consciousness. Though my world during those formative years was largely one of physical enjoyment, subtle influences were seeping into me as surely as water seeps into thirsty ground, penetrating every fiber of my being, coloring every reaction.

Once during a violent midsummer storm, the sky grew black as night and flashes of lightning sliced their jagged way through it, thunder pealed and rolled ominously, and at times there was an awesome and frightening stillness. Sheltered between the huge buttressing roots of a big pine, I lay there waiting for the wind to strike. It came in an all-engulfing roar through the high tops, and as the pine swayed, its roots moved too. The gale increased, the great trees bent to and fro and the earth trembled beneath them. There was a tremendous crash as one of the largest lost hold and fell, the ground shuddering with its impact. Then another leaned nearby and I watched as it slowly moved downward, bringing with it a shower of bark and branches. At that moment I knew fear and wonder and an inner exaltation I was to know again and again through life, a sense compounded of being one with the elements, the trees, and the wild forces they bow to.

Long afterward in the high Sierras I understood what John Muir felt when he climbed a tall spruce during a storm and hung there, as he said later, "like a bobolink on a reed . . . taking the wind into his pulses," part of the wild music of the storm.

I knew it during a hurricane in the great cypress swamps of the South, among the old beeches of Sherwood Forest in England, and once in the Black Forest near Heidelberg when all the powers of the *Götterdämmerung* seemed released, and when camped beneath a stand of huge spruces on the Hayes River near where it flows into Hudson Bay.

That day, with an arctic wind sweeping inland from the ice flows of the straits above, it was so bitterly cold we could paddle only a few hours at a time without being forced to land and build a fire. By nightfall, wet and tired from many rapids and portages, we dragged our gear into the shelter of a dense grove of spruces and pitched our camp in an opening beneath them. Only when the fire blazed high did we discover the enchantment of the place we had found, a high-ceilinged room with a golden floor and golden rafters, the walls huge black boles of trees. Not a gust or breath of wind disturbed us as we lay basking in the warmth. The spruces moved and groaned, but we were safe from the storm, safe and snug as animals in a cave. The day's adventures, the roaring rapids, loss of equipment, the struggle against the wind and sleet were far away. We ate our food, got into the sleeping bags, and watched the firelight on the canopy above us.

While great trees have fascinated me since early boyhood, they were only a part of my experience, for ponds and swamps, beaver flowages and backwaters have also haunted me. Beginning perhaps during the time of the alder-thicket hideaway near home, as I roamed farther afield I found this was merely a start, that its tiny glistening pools extended into myriads of larger quiet waters in river mouths and unending bogs. Sunrises, sunsets, and even sounds were different there, the whispering of grasses and wild rice, the wings of ducks, the mysteries of mists and shrouding fog.

It was no wonder that waterfowl became important to me during the days of my hunting. By the time I acquired a small shotgun, I had already explored the marshes nearby, stalked the edges and practiced on coots and rails, but I wanted a mallard above all, a drake with a green head and blue wingbars shining in the sun. One morning just at dawn I pushed my canoe down the winding channels of a slough, slipping silently from bend to bend. Muskrats crossed before me and I marveled at the sculling of their tails, beaver swam by dragging branches of aspen for their winter food, mud hens skittered ahead and I was tempted, but held my fire.

I moved around a bend and there before me was the mallard of my dreams in the very center of a placid pool. It seemed enormously large, a lone drake, its green head shining in the sunlight. I did not move, let the paddle slide noiselessly into the water. Every detail of that moment was etched indelibly in my memory, reflections of alder and willow, a golden tamarack like a spear of light, yellow reeds around the rim, the great bird part of its own reflection.

The mallard did not stir, not a tremor or quiver of its wings, nothing to indicate the hidden tenseness of powerful muscles preparing for flight. I reached for the gun resting against the thwart, moved as though in slow motion, my whole being concentrated on what I must do.

The scene exploded in a rush of wings as the drake climbed into the sky. My gun followed, and as the bird leveled off, I fired. To my utter amazement it collapsed and struck the surface of the pool in a shower of golden spray. Grabbing my spare paddle, I pushed over swiftly and lifted the mallard into the canoe. For a long time I sat looking at the bronze of its breast, the greens and blues of the wingbars, the pearly white of the underside. I felt no remorse, only wild happiness and joy. The bird before me was part of the marshes, the dank smells of shorelines in the fall, of all the waiting and hoping I had done.

Fifty years later I stood at the marshy entrance to the old Lake Superior slough I had known as a boy. The dirt road and wooden bridge were replaced by a modern highway skirting Chequamagon Bay, cars and trucks whizzed by, but miraculously there was no other change. A flock of ducks floated offshore and I saw them against the sunset as they rose. In a flood came the memories of early days, bluebills coming in with the sound of tearing canvas, the whisper of wings over rice beds, and the slow, lazy quacking far out in the dusk, ducks against a thousand rosy skies, the clamor of geese flying out of the north, the drifting of the first snow flecking white against the brown leaves of alders and rushes, horizons fading into swirling storms, and before the freeze-up the high sound of whistlers heading south. My hunting meant all that, and now as I looked back from this long-remembered place, I realized that without my vast complex of treasured experiences, the work of preservation of all wild creatures and their native habitats might not have been as vital to me were my dreams not haunted by their beauty.

Looking out toward the open bay that day I watched the lights come on at Barksdale, Washburn, Bayfield, and the lighthouse on Long Island marking the sandy reef guarding the entrance to the Apostle Islands, the wide-open sweep of Lake Superior beyond them.

Long Island was the first I came to know. In the spring when arbutus bloomed, whole slopes were rich with the smell of them, and in late summer they were blue with berries. Seagulls always called and wheeled off the beaches, and there was a whispering in the sands. It was an isolated world different from the woods and marshes, far enough from the mainland to give it a sense of remoteness. While ships passed its tip, they did not stop, but stayed well away from the danger of its reefs.

Once I was marooned there alone during a storm when my companions failed to return. I had no food but berries, no shelter except a hollow where the wind could not reach, and I waited out the gale thrilled as I had never been. That island of long ago was my ship, and I sailed it through the hissing combers toward the blue horizons of the open lake.

Since then I have known many islands, among them Cumberland, one of the Golden Isles of the Spaniards off the coast of Georgia. It has twenty-six miles of unbroken beach backed by dunes with their grasses, scrub pines, and palmettos, and the burrows left by the first Spanish explorers. There are huge live oaks inland, always birds and the winds. Then there is a barren island in Great Bear Lake close to the Arctic coast of Canada, glaciated granite painted with orange lichens, a lone cluster of scraggly, dwarfed spruces bending away from the wind, some prostrate on the rocks. There are others in unnamed lakes and along forgotten seacoasts, most of them windswept and in the teeth of storms, their living dunes grown with heather and willow and ghost trees and the eternal grasses holding the beaches against the blasts from the sea. Some are little ones, tiny bits of rock tucked into hidden bays, grown with wild flowers and loved by the birds.

Why such places held me in my youth and all my life I do not know, unless my forebears along the Viking coasts of ancient Scandinavia were so much a part of howling gales and fogs, of bitter winds and the bleak barrenness of granite, that their legacy of terrain became my own. Long Island in Lake Superior was a coming home for me, and so it has been with all the islands I have known. Boone in his dark and bloody ground knew nothing of such places, nor did the others of his breed. Theirs was a different wilderness from mine.

In me was a growing consciousness of beauty. Wilderness to those of another age was a threat, something to be overcome and endured, and while there is no doubt of their love of unsettled country, it is doubtful if many saw it through the eyes of appreciation. While I may have come to this through the gradual development of awareness, I know now that the reading I did played an important part.

A paragraph of Henry Van Dyke's describing a rapids in the moonlight impressed me greatly. I read it over and over until it became part of my own vision. Even now as I say the old familiar lines, I realize they opened up a world of beauty and meaning beyond the purely physical.

"The full moon climbed into the sky as we sat around our campfire and showed her face above the dark pointed tree tops. The winding vale was flooded with silver radiance that rested on river and rock and tree trunk and multitudinous leafage like an enchantment of tranquillity. The curling current and floating foam, up and down the stream, were glistening and sparkling, ever moving, yet never losing their position. The shouting of the water melted to music in which a thousand strange and secret voices, near and far away, blending and alternating from rapids to rapids and fall to fall, seemed like hidden choirs answering one another from place to place."

I thought the phrase "like an enchantment of tranquillity" was the loveliest thing I had ever read, though I am sure the first time I was aware of it I probably had to look up the words "enchantment" and "tranquillity" before I could even vaguely have any understanding. Time and again I would go to some little stream in the moonlight and repeat those lines of description.

There were others, the English and American poets, Thoreau, John Muir, Burroughs, and Hudson, and though I did not comprehend it all, the thought began to dawn that in my love of wild places and physical adventure was a deeper, more satisfying feeling I had not known until then.

While those early years seemed dominated by the importance of doing, contacts with other minds introduced me to a new world, driving a wedge into a rift that would widen and make me think more like the poets and philosophers than a hunter and a woodsman. This did not come easily, and there were years when the outcome of the ancient battle between the primitive and a dawning hint of cultural understanding was in doubt; it seemed as though all that was important was what I did and saw. Had the poets not been with me, I might have gone the other way, taken the well-worn trail I already knew.

I emerged from my Daniel Boone period with countless memories and a new dimension to my understanding, a beginning awareness, perhaps, of the real meaning of what I had known, a feeling that getting game or fish was only incidental to the lasting enjoyments of the mind. Recollections merged gradually into a broad montage, became, in a sense, part of an almost forgotten unknown. It was as though my roots had become so firmly entwined in the whole spectrum of wilderness experience, so entangled and utterly dependent upon it, that no matter how distant I might be from the scenes of my boyhood, these ties could never be severed.

The sounding cataract
Haunted me like a passion: the tall rock,
The mountain, and the deep and gloomy wood,
Their colours and their forms, were then to me
An appetite; *a* feeling *and a* love.

WORDSWORTH

CHAPTER III

FEEL OF
THE LAND

AMERICA IS STILL CLOSE TO THE FRONTIER,
so close in fact we can almost hear the rumble of wagon
trains heading west. Burning leaves in the dusk of Indian
summer bring memories of times when skies were red from
prairie fires and flaming woodlands along the routes of migration. Far horizons thrill us as they did then, the blue and
white of distant mountains, the reaches of open space on
deserts and plains. In the mists of morning along our rivers
and lakes, ghosts speak to us of unnamed waterways flowing
clean and full to the sea.

When we cross the great plains it may be hard for Americans to remember soil that had never known a plow or vast herds of buffalo, though this is part of our recent past. While our way of life has changed, there is within us a feel for the land and what it used to be. It is part of our bone and sinew, part of the very air we breathe.

We treasure reminders of those days and over fireplace mantels hang squirrel rifles, powder horns, and bits of pewter to catch the light. At our gates are wagon wheels, though most of us have never ridden anything slower than an automobile. We hang oaken buckets in wells that have never known water, eat, drink, and make love in darkened rooms lit only by candles stuck in wax-encrusted wine bottles. We watch "Wagon Train," "Gunsmoke," and "Bonanza," thrilling to scenes that were real a few generations ago.

We cannot forget, and those days seem to our present frantic era like the golden age, though we know they were fraught with danger, insecurity, and bloodshed. It was a time of high adventure and challenge when one could always move if dissatisfied. Rewards often went to the bold and unscrupulous, and if a man could hold what he found, no questions were asked. There was always new country to the west.

Over the years a growing sense of continental belonging and a fierce attachment to newfound freedoms emerged. Few who followed the long trails remembered much of their European heritage, but they did know that in the old countries there was little chance for betterment or scope for their lives, and that men lived and died without knowing what a life of freedom could really mean. And so whether they were aware of it or not a loyalty was developed to the soil, a loyalty welded by hope and faith, privation and danger, and the terrible effort of wresting farms, towns, and cities from the wilderness. Moderns think they have forgotten and in their urban lives have no need of this past, but deep within them is a smoldering nostalgia that can burst into flame should existence become too crowded, boring, and commonplace.

Those old days were more real to me because of having known life on a northern Wisconsin farm. This was the land of the barrens, sandy glaciated ridges and outwash plains, overlooked while the fertile prairies of the Mississippi Valley were being homesteaded and developed. No one thought of going north into the cut-over pinelands while open land was available elsewhere. Why grub out stumps when there was deep, black, grass-covered soil where buffalo once roamed by the millions. But there came a time even before the turn of the century when men turned to the north to carve out homes from the remaining lands.

It was on such a farm that I worked as a boy, got the feel of land that had never been broken to a plow and a hint of what pioneering meant. I did not know at the time that this area was one of the final remnants open for homesteading in the midwest, and that eventually many of the farms being grubbed out of the slashings left by logging would be abandoned and returned to the forests from which they came. To me it was still the old frontier and land of opportunity with challenge and work for men.

Soren Uhrenholdt with his wife Kristine, both natives of Denmark, had taken a homestead along the Namekagon

River, and with their family of four boys and four girls, one of whom became my Elizabeth, were then working out their destiny. One Sunday morning Dad Uhrenholdt and I climbed a high hill south of the farm where we could look down into the valley.

"Remember the first time I came here," he said. "Didn't know where I wanted to settle until I could see it all."

Below lay the Namekagon country. There were scattered fields and many patches of pine with a white farmhouse on a knoll gleaming in the June sunshine. It lay there before us fresh and sparkling and the air was full of the music of whitethroats, song sparrows, and robins.

"It looked different then," he said. "No fields, just stumps and brush as far as I could see, all except the clearing with a frame cabin in its center. There were young pines around it, a good stand of them along the river and just below the house a solid grove the lumberjacks had left because the trees were too small. The big timber was gone, but when I saw those young trees, I knew that someday they would be tall and straight. Other crops grow quickly, and when they're harvested, the soil lays bare. Trees are different, grow more beautiful with the years."

Then he told me of his dream, how each field would have its setting and be a picture in itself.

"Mother and I felt that a farmstead should be more than a place for the raising of crops and cattle," he told me. "It should have character and beauty. And we knew the pines, if they were taken care of, would give it both—a place our children would love."

I could see his plan taking shape, a clump in a corner, a shielding growth north of the house, a spearhead cutting into the meadow. The farm seemed cradled in pines as though the fields flowed into them in a careless unplanned symmetry of their own.

From that day he and I had an understanding about many things that had little to do with the practical aspects of farming—the dew on a field of potatoes in the early morning, the way of sunlight through the needles of great spreading branches, the feeling of having strong trees around us.

He taught me that hard physical work was rewarding to body and mind and that building a farm and saving the beauty around it was one of life's greatest satisfactions. I know now that this could have come in no other way than by actually playing a part in the development of the homestead and through such primitive challenges as wresting a swamp hole from a raw and ragged clearing, plowing it for the first time, harrowing its rough furrows and dragging until they were smooth, endlessly picking stones and roots until at last the field lay ready for planting.

One morning he took me to the center of a new clearing and we stood at the edge of a swamp hole, a ragged mass of brush and blackened stumps of tamarack and spruce. There was still water in the bog and around its sodden edges I saw a woodcock boring into the soft mud for worms.

"When you are through clearing," said Dad, "you can plow the field. By fall it should be ready." He left me with a heavy double-bitted ax, a brush hook, and an iron crowbar.

4 3

There was no question in his mind of my ability or strength. Somehow the work would get done.

I was young, my body tough and hard, and the work exactly what I wanted. I started at the edge and began cutting the thick stand of tag alder, willow, and dwarf birch. The ax was sharp, and I watched carefully so I would not hit the rocks beneath the surface. Hour after hour went by cutting the brush and dragging the heavy clumps to a pile for burning.

Working there was only part of the day; we rose at four A.M., spent two hours doing the chores, my part feeding and currying the horses, throwing on the heavy work harnesses, finally cleaning the barn and turning the cows out to pasture. Then a big breakfast with the crew, porridge and pancakes, meat and potatoes washed down with hot, steaming coffee, and out to the fields once more.

I gloried in the long days, enjoying the sweat and weariness. Stripped to the waist, my torso black from charred stumps and logs, often bleeding where the sharp brambles or branch ends had cut me, smelling the smoke and the torn earth, I was glad to be alive. This was a battle, what a body was for. When the sun sank low, it was time for the chores again, and I hated to leave the clearing, and when morning came I plunged into the work with as much enthusiasm as ever. Each day the swamp looked cleaner, and at last all the brush was piled and burned, the biggest roots chopped, and the stumps ready for pulling.

Jens, the oldest son, came with me that day and showed how it was done with a team of logging horses, how to hitch a chain to one of the roots and place the team so it would pull in the right direction. To the big grays it was an old story; they knew from experience what to do. At his command they would lean into the traces and with a tremendous surge of weight and power paw the earth until the stump gave way. Sometimes one was stubborn and the animals fought until they could do no more, stood heaving, flanks wet with sweat and blackened with muck and water. They would back and Jens would try the chain on another root, pulling in a different direction until it all but leaped from the ground. Some larger roots would not give, and these we chopped and left, knowing in time they would rot and break loose. He left me then with a final word of advice.

"There's always a way," he said, "and the horses know. Take your time. There's no stump that can't be pulled if you work at it."

This was exciting and new to me, for each one was different, each a challenge, and I felt the horses enjoyed the work as much as I. When a big stump finally broke away after several tries, they stood there as though proud of what they had done. I would rest them and wait until they breathed easily once more, then drag the monster triumphantly to the edge of the field. As the windrow of huge, sprawling stumps grew longer and longer, it lay like a barricade between the unbroken land and the field being tamed. It was good to look over what we had done.

By fall the swamp hole and the field were ready for the breaking plow, the standing water gone and the sod dry enough so the horses would not bog down. The work had

45

been hard, harder than any I had ever known, but it was child's play compared to what lay ahead. I had never handled a breaker until the time came to plow. It was huge, and heavy as it had to be, twice as large as any I had seen; the great, shining blade had a point of steel as sharp and well tempered as a spear. I lifted the heavy handles, placed the point down carefully into the first clump of sod, spoke quietly to the horses as they leaned against their traces. When I called it went in and we were rocketing across the clearing. Accumulated since the retreat of the glacial ice ten thousand years before, this was the first time it had been broken and turned to the sun. This day I was a pioneer of the North American continent, knew how men felt who plowed the rocky clearings along the Atlantic Seaboard, those who broke the heavy sod of the buffalo country, the valleys of the Pacific Coast. Never again would I feel the same about broken land.

At the end of the row I turned the team so we could see the long, brown furrow we had made. It was not as straight as it might have been, but it was a start, and in time the whole field would lay brown against the sky. Before the coming of the snow it would be ready for seeding in the spring. My weight was barely enough to hold the handles of the plow, and at times I was lifted clear off the ground and thrown from side to side, but somehow my grip was not broken even when we hit roots that stopped us dead, and I would hold on desperately as the horses pawed themselves to a lather until they broke through, or I was forced to get the ax. This was glacial moraine with many boulders; the small ones did not stop our progress, but when they were large it was a different story. The chain would be placed so a rock could be rolled, and many times I had to plow a trench deep enough to cover it. Logs were a special hazard, especially old resinous ones lying crossways of our course. Each furrow was a battle of its own.

For long, exciting days the struggle went on, and I seemed to grow in strength and wisdom in the ways of handling difficulties and working with the team. Though wearied and sore by dusk, it was a good tiredness, and toward the end I felt as though I could go on forever. Then one afternoon just before sunset, the entire field was plowed, the swamp hole merely a dark depression in its center. The windrow of stumps lay stark against the sky, the scraggly roots evidence of the war I had waged. That night I rubbed down the team, gave them an extra and well-earned ration of oats, patted them as they munched contentedly in the darkness.

The field did not belong to me, but I had helped make it, and like all pioneers, I longed for fields of my own. Someday I too would own land, build a home, have horses and cattle. Nothing could be more satisfying, nothing more worthwhile, a dream I had never known before. During those formative years I knew the hopes and satisfactions of a homesteader on a bush clearing in the north, a young man taking his place on the old American scene as hundreds and thousands had done since the days of discovery; but more important than all else was a growing feeling for the land itself.

There were so many things to remember from that experience, a veritable flood of indelible impressions, white mists of morning above a meadow, the light as the sun burst over a notch in the distant hills, the rich smells of newly turned earth, the sounds of horses and cattle in the barn at night, and the coming in after a long day and washing up at the pump in the glow of sunset. I knew little of the real hardships of the men and women I came to know, nothing of the heartbreak and catastrophies that seemed to dog the settlers wherever they went, but I began to sense what was theirs alone, a welding of their lives and spirits to the soil, something no one could possibly know without having lived with them and shared their vicissitudes.

I learned many things that year, that hunting and fishing were seldom done for sport or relaxation, but for food and during times when nothing else could be done because of the weather. Men did not go to the woods because they needed a change of pace or escape, for the simple reason they were out of doors all the time. The woods, fields, lakes, and rivers were their lives. They felt about game laws as did all pioneers, that those who lived on the land had a right to take what they needed, that regulations were for city folks, not for those who lived back in the bush with larders often in short supply.

Shining deer at night along the edge of a clearing or some lake shore was an accepted way of getting fresh meat. I remember the black silence, the ripple of the canoe, the drifting light, probing, exploring, playing on bushes, trees, and stubs—the golden gleam of eyes—the canoe moving toward them—paddles never out of water—the ears, the head—the steady glow. We were alone in a dark, primeval world—no sound but our heartbeats, our breathing—a hundred feet, fifty, forty, the canoe moving on its own, floating toward the balls of fire.

The head is high, ears swiveling, body tense. The darkness explodes with a roar. The animal falls into the water, threshes violently. We push forward, dispatch it, and haul it onto the bank, then into the canoe, and head for a little island. We dress it there, wash it out, and lay the carcass on a fresh carpet of ferns on the bottom of the canoe.

The silence descends again and an owl hoots back in the timber. Our work is done and we are proud, we have food that will be welcome. It never occurred to us that what we had done was wrong, and were no more worried than the buffalo hunters of the plains before the coming of the law. We were the same as they, the meat was ours to use.

My best friend during those early days was Dewey Sabin, the son of a logger living on a bush farm in the Totogatik country a few miles to the north of the Uhrenholdt homestead. Beyond Dewey's home was nothing for forty miles or more, only trails left from the logging, no other developments or habitations. This wilderness was ours and we cruised it as we pleased. Dewey was a superb woodsman and taught me where the tote roads went, the location of springs, creeks, and little lakes, patches of virgin timber and trappers' cabins of long ago that would shelter us at night.

A couple of miles to the north and west was the Totogatik River meandering through a great marsh crisscrossed with logs. He and I were the only ones who fished there, no beaten trails along the banks, no broken branches or debris, no competition from others. We used worms and grasshoppers, for we had never heard of flies, and the speckled trout we caught were natives that had never known a hatchery. They were short, heavy, and brilliantly colored.

Along one stretch of marsh, the grass was tall as a man, and we stalked the river, knowing if the bank should tremble or the grasses wave, we would take no fish. Most of the trout were small, eight and ten inches, but sometimes there would be a monster of a pound or two or even three, threshing around on the water. When I dream of trout fishing, I think of what the river was like when Dewey and I were young.

After the crops were in and the first snow fallen was a time of new activity all over the Namekagon Valley in spite of the hunting that had been done, for this was the legal open season, the time to drop all work and lay up as much meat as possible for the winter. At the Sabin home the day began with a big breakfast while it was still dark outside. A dozen men sat around the table, trappers, guides, lumberjacks, and settlers. Dewey's mother hovered over the big, glowing range, brought stacks of hot cakes, platters of fried potatoes and salt pork, and if the season were under way, venison ribs and steaks. There was little talking at the table, for all had worked in lumber camps where silence was the rule, and nothing must interfere with the all-important business at hand, the stowing away of food as expeditiously as possible.

Breakfast over, the hunters took the trail toward the slashings. They knew where they were going, where the drives would be made, who would stand and who would go through the swamps and thickets. When the hunting area was reached, half the crew spread out along the trail for a drive toward the west, waiting until the others had circled around to station themselves on hillsides or openings where the deer might come through. Dewey and I, being younger than the rest, were chosen to stand, so we headed down the logging road for our lookout places half a mile beyond. I climbed onto a big stump on top of a knoll from which I could see for a hundred yards in all directions. By now it was getting light and I checked my rifle and waited.

No one knew the terrible urgency that was mine. A partridge flew up into a tall aspen nearby, balanced itself precariously as it pecked at the frozen buds. A red squirrel chirred and scurried down a jack pine, a pair of chickadees twittered in a bush beside me. Then there was no sound at all, the silence so overwhelming it seemed I could not stand it. For a time I debated whether to change my position to a nearby rock, then decided to stay. The partridge pecked away in the aspen and the squirrel eyed me from its perch, chirring nervously.

Off in the distance the brush cracked sharply. A deer, or one of the drivers? I looked over the white hillside, then down into the valley, hoping against hope. For a long intolerable moment there was no further sound, then crash—and crash again. I became conscious then of a soft, rushing sound as though snow were being brushed off a balsam; I checked the safety of my 30–30. Another crash, closer this time, and the same awful silence, and I knew that whatever it was was watching me.

A woodpecker beat a sharp metallic tattoo on a dead stub and the partridge fluttered noisily to another tree. In the distance something moved, dark against the whiteness. Men did not wear red caps or jackets in those days. A man would be a dark shadow the same as a deer, would move if he were one of the drivers. It must be a deer. It had to be. There was a swish toward the bottom of the gully. A buck would move like that, easing through the brush, keeping away from windfalls. A hunter wouldn't be down there at all, would stay on the side hill working his way to the top of the ridge. I stared into the gully, covering every foot of it as far as I could see. Then right where I had been watching, I saw the animal clearly, a buck with a fine spread of horns slowly working his way toward me, stopping every so often to nibble the tips of striped maple. I aimed at the shoulder, held too long, then to my dismay he faded into a clump of balsam and was gone.

A shallow draw ran from the thicket to my stump. If the buck came out, he would come this way. The balsam branches moved, and I saw him again, completely unaware of my presence. When he was no more than a stone's throw away, I drew a bead on his neck, held my breath, and squeezed the trigger. The deer dropped without a tremor.

Dewey had seen it all and was there almost as fast as I. Together we dressed the animal and hung it in a tree with a red handkerchief to mark it. My buck—the very first. It was unbelievable. It had happened, but somehow the wild excitement was gone. Bugles should have sounded to mark the great event, the fulfillment of the dream I had had so long. All Dewey said was, "Nice shot, you didn't spoil any meat." It was all too commonplace; I had simply hung up some venison for the winter's larder, the sort of thing expected of us on the farm, as much as getting in the crops or clearing land.

At the end of the day one of the men came with a horse and a go-devil sleigh and we loaded on my buck and three others and followed the outfit home. We washed outside, unloaded the guns and stacked them in their usual place against the wall. That night after supper there was much talk about hunting, of seasons past, of deer seen and missed, but I acted as though the buck I shot was nothing out of the ordinary, and certainly not my first. No one patted me on the back or made anything of my kill. What I had done was taken for granted. The fact I had proved myself was known only to me.

The four deer hung head down on the long pole in back of the house, and after supper Dewey and I went out to look at them. Meat for the winter, wild meat to supplement pork and beef.

"There'll be more before we're through," said Dewey. "That's why the pole is twenty feet long."

I walked over and stroked the back of my buck. Not a mark on it, four tines on a side, an eight-pointer, as big as the one I had missed on that trip with Old John.

Some of the men came out, glanced at the deer casually, looked at the sky. "The swamps are froze," said one of them. "Jack will start logging after the season's over."

"He'll need more snow," replied another, then they all went over to the bunkhouse.

North of the Sabin farm was Lake Totogatik, the source of the river we fished, and on its north side was a stand of ancient hemlocks as big in their way as the pine timber of Star

Lake to the east. The huge trees, hung with moss, spoke to me, and I stood among them and repeated some lines I had learned in school:

> "This is the forest primeval
>   The murmuring pines and the hemlocks
>   Stand as Druids of eld."

I knew nothing of Druids in those days, but the poet must have known or he could not have written as he did. Dewey and I went there many times and explored the old stand from end to end. I came to know the hemlocks not only for their hoary beauty, their enormous old trunks, the clean forest floor beneath them, but for the power old trees always had to move me. Feeling as I did, I should have been shocked when Uncle Jack decided to log them, but in the frontier community of which we were a part, it seemed the logical thing to do.

Jack was an old-timer, lithe, lean, and quick on his feet. He knew the logging camps all around and had worked in them since boyhood. There was a lilt in his speech, and the way he could sing "Shanty Boy" would have put modern folk singers to shame. He had lived the life he sang about, learned the songs in the bunkhouses of the pine country, had known the hardships and rewards of working in the woods.

He cut the trees that winter, the last big logging he ever did, and when spring came the ancient stand was gone with nothing left but tufts of brush, the remains of his skid rows, and an abandoned camp. In spite of his apparent callousness in cutting the hemlocks, he loved the country with an abiding passion. He and I made many hunting and fishing trips together, and I learned from him that each one into the woods was an exciting adventure. His was a zest and sense of romance that colored everything.

"I want to die with my boots on," he told me once. "I want to lay down under a pine tree when it's all over, someplace close to the river where I can hear the rapids and listen to the whitethroats. That's all I want."

Not long ago, when he was almost eighty, he did exactly that, and now lies buried where he wanted to be, beside the Namekagon he loved. After his passing I thought of Kahlil Gibran where he says, "For life and death are one even as the river and sea are one and what is it to die but to stand naked in the wind and to melt into the sun and drink from the river of silence." Jack had come home at last, had melted into the sun and drunk of the river of silence.

Most of the old-timers are gone now, but I remember what they taught me, not only of the woods and rivers and of the earth itself, but something immeasurably greater that tied me with them to a forgotten past, a certain sense of belonging, lost in the world of today.

There was Olaf Cook, who showed me how to shoot. While modern sportsmen might smile at his technique, it worked for him, and when after long practice I finally caught on, it worked for me too.

"The first thing to do when you get a gun," he said, "is forget about the sights. Only greenhorns have to aim. Real hunters point." Time and again I watched him make impossible shots at deer going through the underbrush, always a quick point with no attempt to aim.

Years later when I had developed something of the same sort of skill with a shotgun, I wrote a story called "I'm a Jump Shooter" in which I tried to tell how the system worked, the swift almost unconscious correlation between eye, mind, and body that primitives use in throwing a stone, a spear, or a boomerang, an intuitive sort of thing with its origins deep down and below the gray matter of the brain.

A British doctor in the RAF who had studied the characteristics of flyers who became aces wrote me after reading my article.

"When the chips are down," he said, "aces don't have to think. Their reactions are beyond thought and conscious planning. Thinking takes too long. The aces survive while others die."

I don't mean to imply that my old friend Olaf could have been an ace, but his reactions were the same, a finely attuned coordination and almost instinctive accuracy. In any primitive society he would have been a great hunter or warrior. Whether his weapon was a gun or a bow and arrow, it would have made little difference. His breed is gone now and his prowess in providing game forgotten. Daniel Boone, Kit Carson, Jim Bridger—he epitomized them all. The sound of his 30–30 has long been stilled, but when I hear the guns again as I did this morning and see the first snow on the ground, it seems as though he must be back in the hills somewhere.

There was something hard to define in Olaf, a sort of

authenticity and realness that was part of the pioneer experience. So closely interwoven was he with all of it that I never think of hunting or see hunters going forth with their high-powered cars, rifles with telescopic sights, orange-colored jackets, and modern camping equipment without remembering.

Charley Hoffman gave me the same feeling about trout fishing. He liked to fish the Namekagon at dusk and waded without benefit of boots, used flies he had tied himself, and usually came back with a basket full of speckles. He taught me how to stand motionless long enough to become a part of the river.

"Don't go running around," he said. "Be quiet and wait for the trout to begin rising. Make them think you're a rock or a log and you'll get plenty. And when you make a cast, let your fly drop like it's alive, fluttering a little with one wing up and the other down."

I never did reach Charley's perfection, but I learned to be quiet, so quiet one night that a hunter working his way down the river spotted me standing near a clump of alders and stalked me as though I were a deer come down for a drink.

A trout had been rising just below, and one of the flies Charley gave me was drifting toward the circle of ripples. Out of the corner of my eye I saw the hunter rounding the bend above, but was so intent on the rising fish, I never dreamed he was watching me. The speckle rose and took the fly and I played it carefully, finally brought it to my net.

It was then I saw the hunter very close now, watching

my every move, his rifle pointed toward me. At first I could not believe he might think I was a deer, then I knew and yelled.

"Could have sworn you were a deer," he stammered. "When you flicked those mosquitoes away, I saw the ears, and when you touched the alders, that doe was leaning down to drink."

That hunter was a young friend and like an Indian in the way he roamed the bush, one of the best woodsmen I ever knew. These were the frontiersmen who filled my memories for years long after the legendary characters were gone. They were the same breed, and from them I absorbed some of their attitude toward life, wild country, and the land itself. Since then I have known many others, in the mountains of the west, in the far north of Canada, the Yukon, and Alaska, but these men in Wisconsin were the first to leave their mark upon me, for they were real and I had lived with them. Theirs was an earth wisdom, a feeling for the land of all primitive people, seamen who haunt the docks and waterfronts of seacoast towns, peasants everywhere who have never moved or been uprooted from the earth.

Though my land changed from the rolling sandy ridges of north Wisconsin to the rugged Canadian Shield of Minnesota and Ontario, the search has gone on for the same authenticity in people and the country itself. The old way of life may be gone forever, but a deep inherent love survives in many Americans. Those who know cannot hide it, and when they meet others who feel the same, recognition is immediate.

Fifty years after that first summer on the farm, I climbed the hill again. A stand of big pine lay below me and I could see the fields with their border of trees, and those along the river. Some of the old ones had been replanted and would soon be part of the surrounding forest, for farming was almost over in the valley, and the old homestead was completing its cycle.

There was beauty as Soren and Kristine Uhrenholdt had pictured it long ago. I know now that Dad was an artist who painted with grander media than most, with fields and banks of trees, with rivers and creeks, skylines, silhouettes, and traceries of branches against the horizon. The picture took a lifetime, but his dream of beauty lives on in the Valley of the Namekagon.

The North Country is a siren. Who can resist her
song of intricate and rich counterpoint—
the soaring harmonies of bird melodies against
the accompaniment of lapping waters, roaring
cataracts, the soft, sad overtones of pine boughs.

Those who have ever seen her in her beauty or
listened to her vibrant melodies can never
quite forget her nor lose the urge
to return to her.

GRACE LEE NUTE

CHAPTER IV

SONG OF
THE NORTH

THE SONG OF THE NORTH STILL FILLS ME with the same gladness as when I heard it first. It came not only from the land of the Great Lakes, but from the vast regions beyond the Canadian border. More than terrain, more than woods, lakes, and forests, it had promise and meaning and sang of the freedom and challenge of the wilderness. I seemed drawn in its general direction as naturally as a migrating bird is by unseen lines of force, or a salmon by some invisible power toward the stream where it was spawned. Within me was a constant longing, and when I listened to this song, I understood.

There was hunger not only to live in the north, but to know about it, its physical character, people, and the creatures that lived there. I felt I must be on a first-name basis with flowers and trees, birds, fish, insects, and mammals, even the rocks and lichens of its hills and valleys, must know this country and so completely identify myself with it there would be no question of my belonging. I wanted to feel as other creatures did instinctively, that this terrain was mine, and that any place I chose to go was where I belonged.

Not only did I want to share it with all forms of life, but with anyone who would listen. I recall my childish excitement in telling about the first flowers one spring and my joy when I learned what they were. This was an ever present urge within me just as it is with those who are fiercely attached to a country that means more than anyplace else on earth. Watch Alaskans as they talk about the North Star State when far from home; eyes shine, faces are animated as they picture the mountains, glaciers, and tundras of their magnificent land.

Someone said, "Do not take from any man his song," and when I think of the one I have heard, what it has meant and how it has guided me in whatever I have done, I know this warning is true, for when a song is lost, it is seldom replaced. At least so it has been with me, for over the years it has changed my life and influenced all the major decisions I have made.

During the years at Ashland on the south shore of Lake Superior, I attended high school and spent two years at Northland College, but there was no real consciousness of the north as a place to live. Those days went by as idyllically as the rest of my boyhood, with studies never too important, and most of my leisure devoted to the woods. Only when it began to dawn that the golden age was over for me and that the time had come to leave home for the university did I realize the awful truth. There was never any doubt about going away eventually, but it had always been in the far and distant future.

My father, a Baptist minister, believed there was no question of what a young man should do with his life; it must be dedicated to the welfare of mankind or tilling the soil, never in mundane pursuits having to do with material things. There were only three choices, the ministry, teaching, or farming, and all others were unessential. Though he never urged his sons to go into one or the other, it was always understood, so it was not strange with such a background that spiritual values were the all-important ones. There was never any guidance as I recall, simply that the broad pattern of our attitudes was so much a part of my thinking, I knew intuitively where it would lead.

We lived as many country minister's families did in those days, with few creature comforts or worries about the future. The missionary barrel once a year, donations from members of the church, and a garden plot seemed to take care of all immediate needs, and if at times necessities were scarce, we knew God in His wisdom would take care of His own. Our homes in northern Wisconsin, wherever they happened to be, were always modest and befitting a man of God, but they were full of books, music, and ideas.

There must have been occasions, however, when father looked askance at the roamings of his second son and his complete absorption with the out-of-doors, but if he had any thoughts or forebodings, he said nothing as long as chores and studies were not neglected. My love of nature did not conflict, and when he read such passages at our evening devotions as "Consider the lilies of the field, how they grow; they toil not, neither do they spin," I was reassured. My feeling for the land, for growing things, the sun, wind, and natural beauty were never at odds with the ideals before us.

Unless some part of each day were spent under open skies I was unhappy. Studies, like chores, were something to be done and done well, but my real life was elsewhere. Memories were not of things learned from books, but of broad montages of Lake Michigan off Sister Bay, the rolling surf, crying seagulls and ships, wild flowers along the road-sides in spring, colors blazing in the fall, and the bluish-whiteness of winter's snow. Inland were the vast, cut-over slashings of the pineries, my trail to the hemlock stand and the little creek where I made my camp. Those last forgotten patches of timber were sacred groves to me, peopled with the spirits of the past. On the shore of Lake Superior lay the open expanses to the northeast, the islands beyond Madeline and the endless sloughs of Bad River and Chequamegon Bay. During those carefree years I became part of the north, and the melody I heard was loud and clear.

I remember the heartbreak when I finally left for the University of Wisconsin. Until that fateful day I had not actually faced the finality of going and had nursed the vain hope that something would intervene. As the train pulled out of the station, I sat mournful and alone looking out the window at the familiar scenes I knew so well, the high wooden trestle over the river, the stands of young pine, aspen, and birch, the clearings with trout streams winding through them, ponds fringed with color, sumac flaming from the railroad embankments. I knew I would be back by Christmas, but that day it seemed forever.

During registration I was confused and uncertain, and for some reason thought only of the Namekagon Valley and the dream of having land of my own. I had never really worried about a career or what to study beyond following the general concepts Father had stressed over the years. It never occurred to me that my absorbing interest in nature might be channeled into some field where it could be used, so without more serious consideration, I enrolled in the school of agriculture, a far cry from what the farm really meant, its romance and beauty, and the feeling of being a pioneer.

Through this initial period, I must have been numb with loneliness and longing, for all I could think of was the woods. Gradually, however, new vistas opened up on field trips taken in soils, botany, and geology. Listening to instructors explaining natural phenomena, rock formations, or vegetational types outside the classroom awakened something within me and I began to see the vague outlines of work I could enjoy. Until then I had not pictured what graduation might bring in its wake, but now it seemed that teaching somewhere in the north and near the woods was the answer.

Intrigued with what these young scientists knew, I was

excited to explore with them the mysteries of the out-of-doors, and each time we took to the field, they opened new horizons to me. My knowledge had been one of breadth, color, and feeling, but soon grew in depth as I sensed the reasons and learned the stories of evolution and change.

The gloom lifted as I saw the trail ahead. Advisers talked about the possibilities of county-agent work with the University Extension, but this did not have the appeal of teaching and using observations to illustrate courses. Furthermore, teaching was in the sphere of occupations Father approved. All my woods experience could be woven into the task of interpreting the country, and I would not only learn, but pass on what I found to others. In the background, as always, was the hope of moving north. This was what I chose to do.

Shortly after graduation, I was offered a position to teach agriculture and related sciences in the high school of a small mining town in northeastern Minnesota with the Indian name of Nashwauk. Using a map I discovered it was on the Mesabi Iron Range, completely surrounded by a maze of blue with no roads or settlements beyond. That first look was enough, for those spots of blue were lakes, and the wilderness around them conjured up visions that filled me with anticipation.

No sooner had I arrived than I headed out of town to see what the country was like, climbed a great, rust-colored mound where the gravel, boulders, and low-grade ore had been piled after the surface stripping to expose the beds of iron underneath. As I worked my way toward the top, the dump glowed with orange and yellow in the last slanting rays of sunlight. Below me was the town, a typical mining camp with little box-shaped houses so close together they seemed to touch. Dominating the rest was the school, a large brown building, and two small white churches. There was a single street, lined with the false fronts of stores and saloons, and all around as far as I could see were the scars of open-pit mining, huge excavations, mountainous stockpiles, and brush-covered hills. To the north was a winding dirt road leading out from the range. It was dusk, and as lights appeared and began twinkling over the mines, a red haze covered the grime and raw ugliness and gave it a certain mysterious beauty. I turned and looked behind me. Come Friday, I knew what I would do.

As the week wore on, all I could think of was my coming trip, and when classes were finally over I took my sleeping bag and a little food and followed the road to its end, then struck cross-country into a jungle of burned and cut-over land until darkness made further progress impossible. I found shelter under the spreading branches of a big white spruce, built a tiny fire, and settled down for the night. This was what I had yearned for and was happier than I had been for a long time.

An owl hooted, and the night was filled with rustlings and sounds almost forgotten. Then the brush cracked sharply and I rose to one elbow—a deer—a moose—then a voice.

"Hello, young fellow—what do you think you're doing?"

Startled, I jumped to my feet. Before me was a burly figure, the face hard and lined, eyes crinkly at the corners and all smiles.

6 7

"I'm Al Kennedy," said the man, extending his hand. "Saw your fire from my trail and thought I'd just drop in."

He sat down and I gave him a cup of tea, and he told me about his cabin on McCarty Lake a couple of miles beyond, and of another farther north on a lake he had named.

"You like the bush," he said, poking my fire, "and there's a lot of it here. Drop in on your way tomorrow and we'll have a visit. You must have missed my trail; it's just over the hill and easier going." And then he was gone beyond the firelight. My first meeting with one of the finest woodsmen in the country. It warmed me having him drop in that way, and I knew he approved my Siwash camp.

In the morning I hit the trail early and within an hour was at Al Kennedy's cabin at the end of McCarty Lake. The coffee pot was on, the griddle smoking hot, and we had sourdoughs, venison ribs, and fried potatoes. He told me about the early days, how he had come with the big logging outfits to take out the pine, and when the miners moved in to dig the ore, he had stayed on with them.

"This is good country," he told me. "Lots of lakes and room enough for a man to stretch himself. If you're hungry there's always meat, ducks, and deer, and sometimes a moose, or fish, and with a little garden like I've got, you can raise enough to last all winter. Got some wild rice, too," he added, and showed me a big sack hanging from a rafter. "Picked it myself, parched it like the Indians do. This is the way to live if you like the woods."

I left him then and spent the rest of the weekend exploring the potholes, beaver flowages, and lakes nearby. I did not know then that this was the southern edge of the Canadian

Shield, the enormous formation of igneous and volcanic rock which extends far into the Arctic, its ragged fingers spreading under and over the Mesabi Range, and sometimes bursting through the surface in bold outcrops of granite and greenstone. This country had more lakes and streams than I had ever imagined, wild waters with no roads or shoreline developments, McCarty, Shoal, Kennedy, Crooked, and many with no names at all.

My first field trip was to the Hawkins Mine, a gigantic gash in the earth a quarter mile in length and several hundred feet in depth. I wanted to show my geology class the exposed beds of iron and explain the story of their deposition. The excavation was like a miniature Grand Canyon with the whole story of the geological periods there for the reading. One of the shift bosses watched us with interest, and I asked him if he had ever found any evidence of marine fossils.

"No fossils in this formation," he told us emphatically. "Just iron ore. The sea had nothing to do with iron."

Shortly after that as we examined a thin layer of calcareous deposit between two beds of hematite, we did find fossil remnants of ancient fish, indisputable evidence of the part the seas had played in the concentration of the iron formations being mined. From that moment geology became a living science to my students. I had told them about iron-forming bacteria, and the importance of concentration through leaching. No doubt they believed me, but when they found the fossil fish, there was no longer any question. This they understood and would remember.

During that first fall, I practically deserted the classroom, discovered anew the tremendous value of field observation no matter what the general course work involved. Slides, dissections, and books were vital, but only in reference to the living world; better to know a bird, flower, or a rock in its natural setting than to rely solely on routine identification and description. This kind of teaching had as much to do with awareness and appreciation as the actual accumulation of knowledge. Observations on the ground, I decided, were just as important as laboratory experiments; in fact, they went hand in hand, and one without the other was meaningless to me.

On weekends I moved into the woods with the goal of the cabin on Kennedy Lake, a location which became the base for most of the wandering I did. Built on a rise above the shore, it was low and squat, with broad eaves and two small windows to the south. It had a bunk, barrel stove, table, and pegs for clothing and outfit. Outside was a sawbuck and woodpile from where I could look over the whole expanse of the lake.

It was the first cabin I really knew and gave me a feeling of seclusion and settling into the country. Some ten miles from town, it usually took three hours or more to get there, and after learning the way in, I often arrived after dark. There was always kindling in the stove, and though the temperature was often below zero, in a little while it was cozy and warm. That cabin smelled as it should, the indefinable fragrance of balsam boughs, logs, and oakum, and when the fire roared and the light from the open door of the stove flickered over the walls, I felt like a bushrat a thousand miles back in the sticks.

After supper I would get into my sleeping bag and read by the light of a coal-oil lamp how others felt about the wilderness. I often thought as I lay there of Al Kennedy, for whom the lake was named. Al had killed a man in a drunken brawl one spring when the jacks and river pigs had come to town to spend their rolls. He was convicted and served time, but because there was some doubt as to his guilt, he was pardoned by President Theodore Roosevelt. The tale was a gruesome one, but I was sure he had killed in self-defense, for there was never a gentler soul or one with more genuine love of the woods.

There was a bond between us from the first night he came into my camp under the spruce, a bond that grew stronger and stronger. If London, Seton, or any of the rest had known him as I did, they would have taken him to their hearts. Had they watched him talk to his dog, or during the endless hours when he made friends with the chipmunks, rabbits, and deer around his cabin, they would have seen at once the kind of man he was and the love he bore all creatures.

"If you like the woods," he kept telling me, "you should take a look at the lake country east of the Vermilion Range. You can put a canoe in anywhere there and follow those lakes and rivers up to Hudson Bay or west toward Lake of the Woods and Flin Flon. This is a fine country, but wait until you've been there. Once you've seen it you'll never come back."

There were others with the same stories about the Quetico-Superior. A young mining engineer who had worked at the Pioneer Mine at Ely before coming to the Hawkins said:

"You can spend a whole lifetime exploring that tangle of lakes and never see it all. There's more water than land, and the only way to get through it is by canoe, just one string of lakes after another, one chain north of Knife on the Canadian side, This Man's–That Man's, The Other Man's, and No Man's Lake. They must have run out of names—the craziest country I ever saw."

I studied the maps and knew what they said was true, decided that during the summer I would take a canoe trip into that fabulous area to see it for myself. When school was over in June, I started for the lake country a hundred miles to the east, and with three young friends from the Mesabi Range, put our canoes into Fall Lake just beyond the town of Ely.

It was a rugged land, a veritable labyrinth of lakes, rivers, and forests entirely different from that around Nashwauk. Logging and mining country, with only a few small clearings between the ridges, most of it was still wild and undeveloped. To our amazement, the pines grew on rocky ledges without any soil, some so twisted and contorted it was hard to tell what they were. The lakes had granite shores, high cliffs rising straight from the water's edge, and rocky shelves smooth as floors, ready for our tents beneath the pines. It was a hauntingly beautiful land, and from the moment we started paddling, I realized Al Kennedy was right, and I would never return to the Mesabi.

After three weeks of traveling some of the major routes through the border country, I knew I would follow those waterways for the rest of my life, not only in the Quetico-

Superior, but far into the Canadian north. So powerful was this reaction, and so convinced was I of the ultimate rightness of my feeling, that I decided to return to school and prepare myself for some work that might make it possible to make my living there. I must have more than a bachelor's degree. Graduate work in geology and biology might open the door to a job with the mines, with survey parties prospecting the back country, or with the new junior college being established at Ely. While I hated the thought of leaving, this was the only way to achieve what I had in mind. My love of the woods was stronger than ever, but there was balance now and direction, knowing I would return.

As my work at the university neared its end, I probed every possibility of employment and finally was offered a post as head of the biology department of Ely Junior College. Thrilled with the prospect of actually going there to teach, I accepted with no question as to duties, course work, or salary, convinced that fate had intervened. As soon as I returned I roamed the area, familiarizing myself with rock formations, ponds, and woods within easy reach. By the time classes commenced, I had found enough possibilities within a mile or two to satisfy all needs for field trips. I did not neglect the larger lakes, and on weekends went as far as I could, gradually got to know all the country within twenty or thirty miles. The longer routes would have to wait, but in time I would know them too.

One sparkling October day I took my botany class to a quaking bog. On one side lay a smooth embankment cradling the glacial pothole as with an arm, on the other a tremendous hill of morainic gravel and sand grown with pines. The embankment, or esker, marked the bed of a river that had run beneath the ice, the bog, where a huge block of it had lain long after the glacier's retreat. When it finally melted, there was a deep hollow, the land around smoothed or filled. Full of water for centuries, ten thousand years later it was covered with a springy mat of moss and heather.

As we walked across the smooth brown surface, it gave alarmingly and trembled beneath us. The pines crowded close around, and along its edges were alder and dwarf birch. In the jungle of grasses we found the runways of meadow mice, and in one place a store of carefully gathered seeds. A flock of pine siskins swooped around us, raiding our find, and then flew off to plant them in many places. Squirrels were busy harvesting cones, digging them down into the duff and mineral soil. The forgotten ones might sprout into seedlings, their roots spreading into the mat to give it firmness for the day when the pothole would be part of the surrounding forest.

We learned about the glacial shaping of the area and the plants and animals which over the years had adapted themselves to the habitat, and learned their ecological impact upon it. But more important, perhaps, was the feeling students got of the area itself and of how it evolved.

That winter I met an old prospector who told me about an abandoned gold mine at the west end of Shagawa Lake. "When I first came up here," he related, "there was a gold strike on and prospectors roaming all over. Couple of young chaps found this vein off the Burntside Trail. Can still see 'em the night they came in and laid those specimens of quartz on the bar of the Last Chance Saloon. They were all excited and so was I, for the stuff looked good.

"Went with them next day and followed the road they'd brushed out to the site—a vein two feet thick and ten to fifteen wide going down at a sharp angle. They'd been working for months staking out their claims and making a stockpile. You can't miss," he said, "even though it's all grown over. That pile of white quartz looms up like a snowdrift through the woods."

When the snow was nearly gone, I took my geology class out there and followed the old tote road with high hopes, my young prospectors as excited about the possibilities as though they were in on a bonanza. The first mile and a half was rough, with windfalls across the trail and tangles of alder and blackberry briers in the low places, but most of the going was clear. We watched constantly for the gleam of white through the trees, but saw only the dark-green wall of balsam and spruce. Then the trail began to rise and finally climbed over a hard rock ledge. We stopped and examined it—slate, iron formations, some intrusions of granite with a few narrow bands of quartz. I divided the group and spread the boys out on either side of the trail.

Suddenly someone yelled, "The gold mine!" And there it was gleaming ghostly and white through the trees. We ran to the shaft and found a great mound of milky quartz, beautiful fractured specimens marked with the cobalt blue of copper staining, the corroded gray of silver, even microscopic flecks of gold.

This was the first time any of us had seen a gold mine in the bush, and we pawed over the stockpile, crawled into the shaft, explored the area for hundreds of yards around, found the remains of an old cabin, a rusty stove and boiler, and odds and ends of equipment covered with leaves and grass. We were all prospectors that day, finding the vein of quartz and with pick, shovel, and windlass hauling the precious ore to the surface. Years of heartbreaking work had gone into the venture, possibly a fortune, for the men who had found it half a century before. We felt their excitement at the discovery and sensed their despair when it came to naught.

"The assays were pretty low," the old prospector confided, "too low to warrant development. Can still see those boys when the word came back it was just another hole. They worked the mine a little longer, then drifted off to the outside, dead broke as the day they came in."

As we sat in the spring sunshine gloating over our find and getting the feel of breakup in the north, I told them what I knew, how placer deposits accumulated in the beds of creeks and rivers from the erosion of veins such as the one before us, the heavy gold settling to the bottom and laying the stage for panning. I explained how hard-rock mines meant the crushing and chemical separation of gold from the quartz. The boys listened without a word, studying the precious samples in their hands, but I knew what they were thinking. Here at this old mine of the Vermilion rush, they learned about gold and the hopes and dreams of the men who had listened to its call.

A week later while the creeks were still running full and the lakes turning black and showing open leads of blue, I took my zoology class to Lamb's Creek where it empties into

the north side of Shagawa Lake. I wanted my students to
see suckers and northern pike fighting their way upstream
to a grassy meadow where the bottom was sandy and ready
for the spawning. Below a tiny cataract with a pool at its
base, dozens of fish had gathered waiting for the time to
make an assault. Then, as though at a signal, they swam
swiftly to its head, hurled themselves into the swirling stream
among the rocks. Some would lie in the midst of it gathering
strength for the final surge, and then with a violent effort
try again. Most of them made it, but some floated down,
beaten and scarred by the sharp rocks, to rest in the pool
or drift slowly back to the lake.

I picked up one of the suckers; it was hard and cold as
ice, but the fight was out of it. A mink ran along the bank,
its beady eyes watching. I tossed the fish toward it, and
though the little animal disappeared, I knew it would soon
be back to gorge on the welcome flesh.

Up in the meadow we found great northerns swimming
among tussocks of grass and sedge in water so shallow their
broad backs and dorsal fins stuck out. They had left the
creek and were spawning there, though the water would soon
be gone. Some would be stranded if they waited too long, but
it made little difference, for the prime purpose had been
achieved, and while hundreds of thousands of eggs would be
lost, enough would mature to perpetuate the species.

Spawning in the spring was part of the age-old cycle,
budding shrubs and trees, fiddlehead ferns growing out of
the black muck, mink we had seen, blue mayflowers, golden
marsh marigold, and flaming stems of dogwood, the whole
vast complex of the ecological system of which they were a

part. The feel of spring was there, surging life, sap running in the maples, blisters of resin breaking on the balsams and running down their trunks.

There were times, however, in spite of the stimulation of field trips, when I revolted against schedules and responsibilities and seriously considered abandoning the classroom and heading for the hinterlands where life was less confining. One of these was when Al Kennedy asked me to go with him to the Flin Flon in Manitoba to join the gold rush there and see the country to the northwest. He had gone the year before and returned with tales of gold, herds of woodland caribou, Cree Indians, and Hudson's Bay posts.

He was convinced we would strike it rich if we got there before the rest of the world heard about it, and he knew a hidden creek where the signs were good. All he wanted, said his carefully scribbled note, was a good bow paddler and a grub stake; the rest of the outfit he had. We would start on the Rainy River, northwest of Lake of the Woods, down the Winnipeg to the big lake, then Saskatchewan and the Sturgeon Weir to the Flin Flon, spend the summer and fall there, build a cabin and come out with a fortune in the spring.

The call was upon me and for weeks I thought of nothing else. Torn between decisions, classes and indoors became intolerable, and as spring approached, I did not know what to do. This was my home country now, and with the combination of academic life, contact with young minds, and the opportunity to roam the wilderness, my future seemed full of promise. How could I leave Elizabeth and our two young sons and the home we had established, leave my friends and co-workers and embark on an expedition for a year or possibly two or three, with no assurance we would find what we were looking for? But when I thought of what it would mean to go off on the great adventure, see the far country I had dreamed about and make a fortune as Al was sure we would, I was tempted.

Then one day as I was paddling up the Kawishiwi River and approaching Dead Man's Portage, the answer came. This would not be my only chance at the Flin Flon, for there were many years ahead. I must not leave my responsibilities, had only begun to know the Quetico-Superior, and just skirted the fringes of experience and knowledge. I wanted to be a good wilderness guide and spend summers in the bush working with the men I had met there, getting the feeling that was theirs. Though I was beginning to unravel the geology of this part of the north, in spite of all my exploring I had barely glimpsed the wealth of its flora and fauna, and I knew little of the earth itself and the complex relationships of life in the area. This wanting to know and to identify myself was an absorbing quest as real and as much a part of the north as the Flin Flon country.

With Al Kennedy there was no choice; he must go while there was time. The following summer he took off with another partner, and that was the last I heard of him for several years. There was no fortune in the gold fields for him, but I knew this made no difference, for he had gone and listened once more to the song of the north he had followed all his life.

Something lost behind the ranges,
Something hidden, go and find it.
Go and look behind the ranges,
Something lost behind the ranges,
Lost and waiting for you. Go.

                                                    KIPLING

CHAPTER V

BEYOND
THE RANGES

WHEN I BECAME A GUIDE IN THE QUETICO-
Superior, I did not realize what it would mean beyond sat-

isfying the urge to see new country. True, I had lived close to the woods and relatively unsettled areas most of my life, but there was something that could not be absorbed on short forays limited to weekends or occasional camping trips during the summer. What that early period lacked was the overall cumulative impact of being away for weeks or months at a time. I needed to know what it was like to work in the woods with constant searching for the same down-to-earth authenticity I had found on the homestead in northern Wisconsin. I felt that only by knowing the men who made their living there could I ever really understand and catch the full flavor and meaning of the land itself.

After the guiding season was over, these men worked in the logging camps or in the mines, ran trap lines, or did some outlawing if the price of beaver was right. I would return to the classroom and, like them, dream of the spring breakup when the lakes would open and we could take to the canoe trails again. The fact I came from the outside was against me, I knew, but I was confident I could prove myself and be as resourceful and competent as they.

When I came to Ely, I had two summers of canoe travel behind me, and while this was only a start, I began exploring all the lakes within reach until I felt more at home. Much of the country, especially on the Canadian side of the border, was poorly mapped, and I learned by trial and error how to find my way. All large lakes had connections of some kind with others, sometimes rivers, often little creeks, or in some cases merely seepages through sand and gravel. The

secret was to find where the water moved, a matter of studying the horizons to determine their lowest points. Black ash,
alder, and muskeg often gave them away, and after a time
it became second nature knowing the way to go. There was
evidence of portages, indistinct and grown over with brush
and blocked by windfalls, but the old trails traveled by Indians for centuries and by prospectors and trappers before
me, were there.

I vividly remember my first long trip beyond the border,
the sense of unlimited waterways and space, the feeling of
being able to travel anywhere if there was enough water to
float a canoe. I learned the locations of smooth, glaciated
shelves of granite, campsites for which the country is famous,
kept in mind vistas of sunsets, moonrises, protection from
prevailing winds, discovered such places were few and far
between, and that it was well to have them in mind and
spaced no more than a day's travel apart.

A good supply of firewood was important, for it was em-
barrassing to have to look for wood after camp was made.
In tree-covered terrain it might seem ridiculous to have to
search for fuel, but there are places where everything is
green and where there have been no forest fires or blowdown
for long periods, or where Indians or others have picked
them clean.

Most parties came for the fishing, and I learned that
trout thrive in deep, clear water and on rocky bottoms, that
in the spring they can be caught off shallow reefs where they
have spawned; walleyes need rocky shores and reefs, but not
the extreme depths of trout; great northerns like weedy bays,

bass smaller ponds with dark waters bordered by lily pads and windfalls along the shores. Some of the larger lakes had all four species, each in its own particular environment. All this was stock in trade.

I knew the haunts of moose and deer, nesting places of herons, ospreys and eagles, beaver dams and flowages that connected lakes, the places where mink, otter and muskrat lived. I found the cliffs where Indian pictographs had been painted by ancient tribes, sites of old villages and trading posts, steeped myself with the kind of information I believed my parties would want. My background of woods experience helped, for the land and all its creatures were old friends.

I practiced using all the cooking information I had, made pan bread or bannock, even cakes and pies in a reflector oven, steaked and broiled fish, and made various stews and combinations. There was much to learn, especially from the guides I met, for they had become expert chefs, an entirely different role than satisfying one's own hunger.

These men, it seemed to me, had been everywhere, to the Sioux Lookout country in the north, down the wild, roaring Albany northeast to Hudson Bay, and to the fabulous gold fields of the Flin Flon in faraway Saskatchewan, casually mentioned names that filled me with excitement, the open doors to a vast and unknown world. The more I heard of these places, the more powerful grew my longing, to see not only all the lakes and rivers along the border, but the uncharted regions of the whole Hudson Bay watershed and the Northwest Territories of Canada as far as the Arctic Coast.

I wanted more than the actual guiding; I needed to know these guides and their feelings about the country they had explored, what motivated them and why they lived as they did. They were a breed apart, as distinctive in their way as the cowpunchers or mountain men of the west.

One was Buck Sletton, newly out of the U.S. Marine Corps, big and burly with a wry sense of humor that colored all he did. No trip was serious as far as he was concerned; he made money at poker, badgered his crew unmercifully, made them feel each trip was a hilarious adventure, that loafing and having fun was far more important than scenery or fishing, and that anyone was insane to work if he didn't have to. His trips were always short, the portages easy, his cooking nondescript, but his parties loved him and swore they had never had a better time.

Arne was a little squint-eyed Finn not much more than five-foot-six, weighing about a hundred and forty pounds; though slight of build, he was all wire, nerve, and sinew. To look at him you wouldn't think he could be much good on a portage, but that body could carry a heavy pack and an eighteen-foot canoe, a load weighing close to two hundred pounds, without strain or apparent effort, the only trace a tightening of muscles along his lean jaws. He rarely said much, was efficiency itself, a good cook, and always knew where the best fishing was.

Gunder Graves, a lumberjack who stayed on after the logging, dressed as all the jacks did—highwater pants, a round, black felt hat cocked just so—and had an air about him of all river pigs of those early days. Tall, angular, and ruggedly handsome, he was more at home with a double-bitted ax or a peavey than with a paddle, but had taken to the canoe trails as though he had never done anything else.

Then there were Frankie and Steve Mizera, brothers who often guided together. Of Yugoslavian descent, their families came to work in the iron mines at Ely. Raised close to the wilderness, they moved into it as naturally as their forebears into the mountains of their homeland. They were much in demand, and in their swarthy compactness and love for the woods, they looked like the Frenchmen who had preceded them.

Matt Heikkila, the very first of them I met, was down to meet the train when I came to Ely. I have never forgotten him; the broad-rimmed hat, pants stagged halfway to the knee, high cheekbones and slit eyes, deeply tanned, with a look of power and poise about him—to me he was the epitome of all woodsmen in the north.

A mixture of nationalities, these were not settlers, for there were no homesteads to open up as in the country to the south. Loggers, miners, and trappers when there was no guiding, expert canoemen, resourceful, and with a lusty sense of humor, they were in a class by themselves. As one said, "Anywhere I hang my hat is home to me," an attitude that prevailed with all of them as long as they had an outfit, some grub, and a party to guide. This same sense of being happy anywhere in the bush I have since found in the far north and in Alaska. An old sourdough summed it all up when he said in telling about his travels, "No matter where you go—there you are."

Over the years they had developed a certain woodsman's dress, not consciously, for they had no guile or flair for romanticism. What they wore was proved by time in mining and logging camps from the coast of Maine to the pineries of the great lakes. Boots were the famous Jefferson Drivers with ten-inch tops and hobnailed soles that made their mark on the river drives, pants usually of heavy duck, fringed and stagged halfway to the knee, a broad belt with a sheath knife, a checked woolen shirt, and a weatherbeaten hat. For bad weather there was always a plaid jumper, but no fancy rain shirts, tightly woven windbreakers or anything resembling modern gear. Their personal outfits were as simple. Guides had no tents for themselves, slept under the canoes, were seldom supplied with sleeping bags, tarps, or mattresses. Such things were for city men, not for men of the bush.

These were the men I wanted to know and work with. Though they put on a show of guiding solely for the wages involved, within each was a deep need that kept them on the trails year after year. Counting the days until they could head back to town, once there, with a drink or two under their belts, a meal someone else had cooked, and a night's sleep in a bed, it soon palled, and they were ready to head back once more.

I met Arne once after a three-month trip toward Sioux Lookout and Lake St. Joe. He came in ragged, hard, and loaded for bear, laughed as he unpacked his outfit and stowed it away. "I've had all the bush I want for a while," he told me. "I'm going to take it easy and sit for a spell."

The very next day he confided almost sheepishly he had an old party going out. "I didn't want to go," he said, "but you just can't turn 'em down," and as he worked away at a new grub list, he whistled softly to himself. And so it was with the rest; the only griping was when they had to wait too long between trips.

Half a century ago the Quetico-Superior was a man's country, with women and children and family groups never straying far beyond the little vacation resorts near town. All parties hired guides, for the interior maps were sketchy at best with blank spaces no one had ever bothered to fill in, and it was a common boast that to the north, outside the thin lines of steel of the Canadian railroads, there wasn't a town or road as far as the north pole.

Beyond the Quetico was a vast lake region of black spruce bogs, with birch, aspen, and balsam on the highlands and scattered stands of pine. This was moose country, and until the turn of the century, woodland caribou. Great gray timber wolves, marten, fisher, and beaver were everywhere in this labyrinth of waterways, rugged canyons, and boulder-strewn valleys. It was a beautiful land with a fatal charm for all who knew it.

This was the wilderness canoe country, and because the guides were the only ones really familiar with it, they met their parties nonchalantly, sure there would be no arguments about routes or procedure. Theirs was complete assurance, and men coming in for trips sensed it, accepting immediately and without question decisions as to what to take or leave behind. To discard some precious item that had been chosen with care and much expense for this special expedition was often a heartbreaking experience.

I can see Buck looking disdainfully at an extra pair of new boots and, without saying a word, tossing them into the discard pile. "If you want to pack 'em over the portages," he would say, "it's your funeral."

That first spring at Ely when I was hoping to get a guiding job with Wilderness Outfitters, I watched the guides getting ready, and marveled at the ease with which they whipped unwieldy mounds of food and equipment into convenient loads for canoe travel. First the empty packs were laid out with a blanket or two in back for cushioning. The cooking outfit went into one, the bag with the nesting pails, the one for knives, forks, and spoons, another for the frying pans, with plates, dishups, pot covers, and cups nestling snugly inside them, the ax with its leather sheath tucked into one corner, the reflector oven always against the back. The tent would go into the pack with the tarps, neatly folded or rolled. Each man had his own personal pack and woe to him if he had more than it could hold. This taught him more about what he could take along than any amount of ribbing, for it was his, and anything extra, tackle boxes or rods, he carried in his hands. The food took up most of the weight in the bottom of each precious pack, and safely against a blanket went the canned goods, and on top, the softer rations, sugar, flour, rice, and beans. Slabs of bacon made good back rests, took the curse off sharp-cornered tins and bits of equipment.

It seldom took a guide more than an hour or two to get his outfit ready, and when he was through, everything was neatly piled and tagged. The pack was known as the Duluth, developed during the days of logging and prospecting in the lake states; easy to throw into a canoe and easy to take out, it was ideal for this type of travel, and on the portages with the leather tumpline as a concession to the voyageurs of old, it never needed improvement.

Most of the guides, I found out, knew only a few major routes when they began, relying on their intuitive knowledge of where the rivers ran as they went along. During the two summers I had traveled the lake country, I learned as they, by dint of much sloshing through bogs, climbing hills and trees, and cutting trails through the woods. This was more important in those days than having maps, for in areas where there seemed to be as much water as land, you could paddle almost anywhere and be sure of coming out in the general direction you chose to go. To be sure, they did get lost once in a while, but not for long, for within each of them was a panorama of the country and a general understanding of the terrain that made confusion temporary. It gave me confidence for the time when I would be heading out on my own.

I waited around the outfitting station for a month, hoping the guides might need an extra man, or some party blow in without a reservation, but day after day it was the same, the old ones already spoken for, and though there were only fifteen, there were always enough to go around.

The day finally arrived, and I'll never forget it, the 23rd of June, 1923, almost two months after the lakes had opened up and were free of ice. The whole crew happened to be out when that fateful wire came announcing the arrival of two men on the noon train. I can see Pete and Joe, managers of the outfit, staring hopelessly at the scrap of yellow paper.

"Guess you're it," said Pete with resignation. "You'll have to take care of 'em, two men, ten days, three hours to pack."

I worked madly throwing the outfit together, laid out the packs, put in the blankets, the cooking outfit, the tent, made out a grub list, checked and double-checked every last item, rolled the glassware, jam, ketchup, and pickles in cardboard strips to prevent breakage, stowed everything away ready for travel, checked an eighteen-foot guide's model Old Town canoe, fitted in a yoke, tested the paddles, found marine glue for patching, put an edge on the ax, saw to buckles and straps, repaired a torn bit of canvas, buzzed around like a squirrel storing cones in the fall, and met the train on time.

At precisely one thirty P.M. it came around the bend as always, but this time whistling and wheezing through the rock cut as though the engineer knew the importance of his cargo. I would take them along the border west to Saganaga, down the Saganagons River to Kawnipi and south through the Agnes-Louisa chain, about a hundred miles all told.

The engine roared into the little station, ground to a screeching halt in a cloud of steam and smoke. The conductor swung off the steps of the lone passenger car and grandly set down the stool.

I tried to appear as nonchalant as the old-timers, hoping no one would guess the wild excitement within me. At the very last two men stepped down, dressed neatly in khaki and high boots; each had a bundle of casting and fly rods. The instant I saw them, I knew it meant a different route.

"All I want is some good bass fishing," said Dave Nelson, the older of the two. "Roger feels the same way, and if we can hit some little bass lakes, that's all we want."

I remembered a lake Walt Hurn, the Canadian Ranger, had told me about east of Crooked, a lake no one fished. We would not go to Saganaga, but down the Basswood River instead, into Crooked, and head north. Walt could tell me exactly how to find it, and if it was good, we'd camp there the whole time and try some of the other lakes nearby.

We got off in the usual flurry of confusion with not a word from anyone that this was my maiden trip. By the time we reached the first portage seven miles from the landing at the end of Fall Lake, Dave and Roger had begun to settle down. Somehow the packs found their way across, clumsily, perhaps, but with laughter and groans and shouts of encouragement. Neither had ever made a portage before, but when I showed them how to throw a pack by balancing it on one thigh, and with an arm through a shoulder strap swing it into place, they caught on quickly. On Newton Lake I could see them begin to work into the rhythm of paddling, and by the time we reached the last portage of the day at Pipestone Falls, they were acting almost like veterans.

Our first camp was on a bare, rocky point in the full blaze of the sunset. I started the fire, put on the pots of water, helped Dave and Roger put up their tent, showed them how to make a bough bed and lay out their blankets, and left them fussing with their tackle.

"When you're through," I told them, as I went back to my fire, "try for some walleyes off the rocks."

While I cooked potatoes and dried fruit and made a pot of tea, they broke out the casting rods. Dave had one immediately and brought it in. Roger followed with another, and before the potatoes were done, had three, enough for supper and to spare. They watched with great interest as I cut around the gills, sliced along the backbone, removing the skin from the steak held flat against the blade of a paddle, and presto, had six glistening fillets all but quivering they were so fresh. I washed them, sprinkled the strips with flour, laid them in the frying pan, and together we saw them change to golden brown.

It was dusk by then, the loons beginning to call, and below us we could hear the rush of Pipestone Falls, and far to the north the deeper thunder of Basswood. They gorged themselves, sat around awhile, then went to their tents and soon were fast asleep.

I learned then that the work of a guide is never done; in spite of weariness, it is his job to do the chores and be ready for an early start in the morning. I did the dishes, picked out what I needed for breakfast—bacon, coffee, cereal —opened a can of condensed milk, and covered the food packs in case of rain. I put a few boughs under the canoe, strung my mosquito bar from the thwarts, tucked some birch-bark and dried spruce twigs into the bow where it would stay dry, finally checked the tent ropes, and only then turned in.

The morning was bright and we were under way by seven. Rocky islands sparkled in the sunlight, the breeze was at our backs, and the loons were laughing gaily. We were heading for the Canadian Ranger station at King's Point fifteen miles away to pick up licenses, and visit with Walt Hurn before going down the river to Crooked. Shortly before noon, we saw the tall pines of the point and the log cabin just behind them; a little closer and we caught the gay flutter of the Union Jack. Walt greeted us warmly, made out fishing permits for Roger and Dave, but of far greater importance, gave me my first Canadian guiding license. I looked at it with respect, the seal of the Province of Ontario across the top, and down in the lower right-hand corner, the date and Walt's carefully scrawled signature.

"To get to the bass lake," he told me, "go down Crooked about ten miles and look for a bay toward the east. No one has been in there, but there's lots of big bass, saw them swimming right next to the portage."

We paddled in the direction of the roar of Upper Basswood Falls, made the first carry around them, and five more before we reached Crooked Lake. I was tempted to run a couple of them, but thought better of it, knowing that if anything happened, the trip would be ruined before it began. By midafternoon we were drifting by the bold cliffs of the Pictured Rocks, looking at the Indian paintings and wondering what they meant. We passed Table Rock, where the Chippewa and Sioux had a meeting after one of their many wars, and near dusk found the portage at the end of a swampy bay. By dark we were across, heading for a rocky island a quarter of a mile from shore. It was not a good campsite, but it was late, so we unloaded, dragged our outfit up to where it was reasonably level, and made out as best we could. After a hurried supper we sat listening to the loons. Bass were jumping down at the shore, and that was all we needed to know.

In the morning we found a beautiful island grown with huge pines and a smooth, rocky shelf for our camp. A deer greeted us and bass swam in the lily pads where we landed. As soon as camp was set up we got into the canoe for our first fishing, Dave using a casting rod with a pork chunk, Roger a fly rod with a bucktail.

Dave cast out, allowed the bait to lie quietly for a moment, then twitched it gently. A bass took it with a tremendous swirl, and when the fish felt the barb, it stood on its tail and danced across the water. While Dave was playing his big one, Roger had another on his fly, and the two played together. Before we were halfway around the island, we had taken six, between two and five pounds apiece.

"This is what we dreamed about," said Dave. "This is what we came for."

And so it was day after day, the bass hitting, the lake

all to ourselves. One night, tired of fishing, we went out under a full moon and sang until midnight. We portaged into small lakes nearby, climbed the hills, and picked strawberries on a grassy slope. Before we realized it, the eight days we had allowed were gone. We tore down the tent, packed up, chose a new route for our return, caught some trout in Robinson and Caribou on the way, followed an old outlaw trail toward home. The last portage was a mile in length, but our loads were light and we didn't mind. On a bald surface of rock high above Basswood, we stopped to rest, feasted our eyes on a vista of woods and rocky hills, and in the distance the blue of the lake where we had started our trip.

My first trip completed, come what may, parties would never worry me again. If they were all as happy as this one, guiding would be a joy. In the short space of ten days I had learned many important things, but most of all that friendships ripen swiftly in the wilds.

"We'll be back," they yelled from the platform, and waved until the train went around the bend, and suddenly I felt strangely alone. It was hard to believe that I had never seen them until this trip, and that we had been together only ten days.

Back in the old warehouse, I unpacked my outfit and stowed it away. Buck was in, and Arne too.

"See you brought 'em back alive," cracked Buck. Not a word from Arne, Pete, or Joe, but I had a good feeling inside me, for I knew my first party had been a success.

During those first years I had the good fortune to team

up with several of the older men, and while I was usually guide number two, it gave me an insight into how they did things that could have come in no other way. Each one had developed certain skills, the result of many years of living in the woods. None could explain how or when he had acquired them, but whatever its explanation, it worked, and even as I did, they watched each other until inevitably a guide was a broad composite of the total experience of every man he had been with.

Frank Santineau showed me how to make a warming oven by simply filling the biggest pot full of hot water and putting a covered pan on top. Standing close to the fire, here was one that really worked.

Watching Joe Chosa leave the dock one day I discovered something I did not know, that in paddling one must lean slightly forward, swinging from the hips and using the torso so completely there is actually little movement of the arms. All of them, Johnny Peura, Alex, and Johnny Sansted, paddled the same way, and today I can tell an old canoeman as far as I can see him by the easy way he sits in a canoe.

It was Big Bill Wenstrom who taught me how to throw on a canoe. He didn't tell me, but I noticed the ease with which he did it, the balancing on his thighs, the short kick of the hips, the twist of the arms as the canoe went overhead. It took many tries before I could drop one neatly on my shoulders, but when I was finally able to do so, it was the easiest way of all.

Johnny Sansted, one of the finest woodsmen of them all, taught me to use a paper bag for flouring fish, rather than laying out the fillets and sprinkling them as I had always done. A handful of flour in a bag, the fillets dropped in, a few shakes, and they were ready for the pan without any fuss or waste of meal.

Frank Carney told me to drop a pinch of salt into any dried fruit I was cooking to bring out the flavor, and to add raisins or berries to bannock, a truth I knew with bush rats again and again all over the north.

There were countless little tricks of theirs I used, and over the years of my association I developed a vast admiration for their competence and the discipline that governed their actions. While they might seem brash at times and almost reckless in the chances they took, beneath this façade of bravado was a deep respect for the elements and the forces they must face. To be sure, there were tragedies, as there always are when men face storms and rapids and difficult terrain, but these were the exceptions, and when they happened, all of them mourned and took the lesson to heart. There was the time Johnny Pluth drowned on the Basswood River, and Jack Linklater in Jackfish Bay, and Howard Schaefer in a storm crossing the English Channel. They knew all this and remembered, looked at the skies and listened to the rapids with more knowing.

Gradually the routine of guiding became so much a part of my life, the packing up and heading out into the bush, the adventure of meeting new parties and the happy reunions when old ones returned, that after a time it seemed as though I had never done anything else.

But there was something more I got from them—their

feeling for the land itself. This I have never forgotten, and when cities bear too heavily, I remember the guides of the Quetico-Superior who had no subtleties or hidden purposes, to whom the idea of contracts and influence was foreign, and who were as genuine and down to earth as the rocky shores of the waterways they followed.

Much of the joy of those years was exploring new country, and many of the first trips were just that. Once leaving Darkey Lake north of the border we decided to follow a river running out of it toward the northwest on a hunch that eventually it would drain into one of the larger lakes such as Lac la Croix. At first there were a series of rocky rapids so shallow we had to wade most of the time, the stream crisscrossed and crowded by heavy alder growth and willows. Gradually it slowed into a broad muskeg, winding on and on into the distance, but the water was deep and we paddled around bend after bend. In one shallow place grown with water lilies, we saw five moose, and later twelve, proof they had never been disturbed. As we approached they paid no attention, and only when we were close did they deign to move out of our way. We finally reached a beautiful lake without a name, and following its outlet, emerged in Martin's Bay of La Croix.

Usually it was a different kind of exploring. Whenever we were windbound by rain or storms or when I was not too sure what lay ahead, I would leave the canoes and head for some distant hill to climb a tree and look for a spot of blue. Sometimes the men would come with me, enjoying the adventure as much as I. Once we saw the blue we returned to the canoes, then with saws and axes cut a trail. Those portages were often long and rugged, and frequently they led to little lakes that had no outlets or connection with waters beyond, but the excitement of standing on a shore none of us had ever seen before more than made up for the backbreaking labor of getting there.

This exploring gave me an urge that has never been completely satisfied, a need that carried me into the far north hundreds and finally thousands of miles from home. I realize now what a tremendous privilege it was, how fortunate I was, to have lived at a time when there was still new and unmapped country. To know what thousands of early Americans had done gave me new perspective on the value of wilderness.

Young men today are little different from those who manned the wagon trains or struck off on treks into the unknown only a century ago; they still need to test themselves. To be tough in sinew and mind and scornful of discomfort and ease, no matter if times have changed, is a common asset of youth, and when inexhaustible energy can be spent in travel through relatively unknown country, the compensations are immeasurable. To climb mountains, go through impenetrable swamps and bogs, or cross deserts in the glare of a pitiless sun takes the same stamina as fighting the waves on great lakes, running dangerous rapids, or portaging over treacherous boulders. No matter where they find the challenges, this is what they need.

To handle an ax with power and precision, driving it into the same cut time after time, takes an eye and muscular control; to paddle without effort comes only after thousands of miles of using the whole body instead of the arms; to slice off a fillet neatly takes far more than a sharp blade—it takes the feel of the knife between the flesh and the skin, something one does not acquire overnight.

Buck Sletton once told me something when heading out into a driving rain. "Remember, young fellow," he said, with the old twinkle in his eyes, "remember, no matter how cold and wet you are, you're always warm and dry." I never forgot that advice, for in it was embodied a philosophy of life and a way of accepting the bush and all that it could mean. It involved not only a basic attitude, but the skills required to live comfortably under any and all conditions of wind and weather. To make a dry and pleasant camp in the face of a storm took more than taut tent ropes and knowing the lay of the land, it meant measuring up to a way of life all Americans once took for granted.

Exertion brings vital physiological reactions when there are worthwhile goals to achieve. Without weariness there can be no real appreciation of rest, without hunger no enjoyment of food; without the ancient responses to the harsh simplicities of the kind of environment that shaped mankind, a man cannot know the urges within him. Having known this during a period of life when I could satisfy these needs, I think I understand what wilderness can mean to the young men of today.

I was aware that the physical aspects of guiding were important, and that without a certain competence it could have been drudgery, but there were other influences that had as great an impact on my thinking. One of these was silence. To be sure, I had known it in the past, but not in the way I knew it as a guide, the cumulative effect of days and weeks on end. This was more than temporary release from noise, it was a primordial thing that seeped into the deepest recesses of the mind until mechanical intrusions were intolerable.

There were special places of deep silence, one a camp on a small island above the Pictured Rocks on Crooked Lake, a rocky, glaciated point looking toward the north, a high cliff on one side balanced by a mass of dark timber on the other. Each night we sat there looking down the waterway, listening to the loons filling the darkening narrows with wild reverberating music, but it was when they stopped that the quiet descended, an all-pervading stillness that absorbed all the sounds that had ever been. No one spoke. We sat there so removed from the rest of the world and with such a sense of complete remoteness that any sound would have been a sacrilege. The great mass of the cliff on one side, the gloom of the pines on the opposite shore, seemed to cup and hold it to the point where we were enveloped by a dark curtain that stifled all thought and feeling.

Then the loons would continue their calling, slashing the curtain as though with a knife, only to have it close again and be as darkly mysterious as before. Here was a deep awareness of ancient rhythms and the attunement men seek but seldom find.

There were many such spots; I found them in the morning and at high noon, as well as at dusk, for the time must be right not only for the place, but in the mind of him who listens. Kahshahpiwi had it in a canyon with the long gash of a waterway disappearing into the distance; Joyce, the hidden lake that seemed perpetually in flood; and Caribou at night when the stars were blazing and close enough to touch; but wherever it happened to be, it was the same, the all-engulfing silence of wilderness.

Since then I have searched for it everywhere and found it far from home. I have known it on the rim of the Grand Canyon at sunset when the colors changed from Chinese reds and burnished golds to the soft, dark purples of twilight, when looking down into the enormous chasm one catches the silence not only of the moment, but of the long eons while the Colorado River was cutting its way down to the very base of some of the oldest formations on earth.

Two years ago I walked out on the Sonoran desert at midnight with the stars so bright they seemed like planets close to earth. I had come to listen to the coyotes sing, smell the desert, and catch its feeling. On top of a hill I found a barren ledge from which I could look out across a valley and get a view of the heavens as well. Then began that strange, haunting medley of blended notes I had come to hear, first only one, then several, until the night was alive with music. Suddenly they stopped, and it was the same as when listening to the loons of the Quetico-Superior—the stillness descended.

I thought as I sat there that this was the quiet we knew in our distant past when it was part of our minds and spirits. We have not forgotten and never will, though the scream and roar of jet engines, the grinding vibrations of cities, and the constant bombardment of electronic noise may seem to have blunted our senses forever. We can live with such clamor, it is true, in spite of what assails nervous systems attuned to the past, but we pay a price, and do so at our peril. I think the loss of quiet in our lives is one of the great tragedies of civilization, and to have known even for a moment the silence of the wilderness is one of our most precious memories.

Something else grew on me during those years of roaming and was never fully realized until I had been in the wilderness for a long time. This was the sense of timelessness and order. As I look back and see its first intimations, I understand my almost imperceptible involvement with a way of looking at life that truly had the power of slowing speed.

In town there were always deadlines, a host of things to do, but as soon as the canoes were in the water and heading out, the tempo changed. The guides slipped naturally into their old pattern; the city men, on the other hand, took longer, several days or a week, perhaps, and sometimes they never did succumb to the influence of natural events, which normally set the timetable for any expedition.

The coming of day and night, the eternal watching of the skies, sunrises and sunsets, the telltale story of winds in the maneuvering of clouds, the interwoven pattern of rain and mist, cycles of cold and warmth, even the changing vegetation—all these filtered into their consciousness as they did into mine. Once having lost our dependence on cosmic events, it was not always easy to regain it. While I had sensed its influence long before, the actual comprehension of time being endless and relative with all life flowing into its stream, took more than blind acceptance or a few hours' removal from civilization.

During some of my first trips I used to lay out a definite route of a hundred miles or more, with campsites strung conveniently along it. Not until I discovered I was simply following the routines of the men who had just left the cities and was robbing them of one of the real reasons for going into the bush did I finally abandon firm plans for some we could follow as we chose, living day by day with the vagaries of wind and weather, and not fretting if we failed to make a certain distance.

Once I tried to make McIntyre in one day from Basswood Lake going by way of Crooked, Robinson, and Sarah. Determined to get there by night, I had told my party about the wonderful fishing, trout on the reefs, walleyes off the campsite, a lake within easy reach swarming with largemouth bass. That day we fought the wind, were drenched with rain, passed up campsite after campsite thinking only of our goal, and by late afternoon were only on Caribou, ten miles away. Tempers were short, everyone thoroughly miserable, and regretfully I made camp, hoping to get an early start in the morning and come what may make our objective by noon.

The morning dawned cold and rainy, the wind was in our teeth. We could not go on, so I tried to make the best of it. Toward midafternoon and far too late for travel, the sun burst out; we took the canoes, left our sodden camp, and found a rocky reef with the finest fishing any of us had ever known. It was in the lee and away from the wind, and during the hour we spent there we were so intrigued we forgot all about McIntyre and decided to stay for an entire week.

That taught me a lesson: we could just as well have stopped in any one of the lakes on the way, and would have been happy. From then on my trips were different, and never again did I attempt the impossible to save my pride, or make a schedule more important than enjoyment. As time went on I knew the various routes more intimately and kept a store of surprises in mind, fishing holes, special lunch places, hidden campsites, and things to do when held up by weather. I was pleased to see how happy everyone was once the feeling of pressure was gone, and how much easier to adjust our plans. The wind might come up or change direction, the fish start hitting, the sun come out in time to air blankets and the outfit after several days of rain. Should someone discover ripe blueberries or a hill to climb, the departure might be delayed for an hour or a day.

With this kind of freedom tension and strain disappeared and laughter came easily. Men who hadn't sung a note for years would suddenly burst into song, and at such times I always thought of Buck and his feeling that loafing and having fun was more important than fishing. When one recalls the ages men lived as other creatures with no dependence on set routines, it is not surprising that once the pattern has been broken, men react strongly. No wonder when they return even for a short time to the ancient system to which they are really attuned, they know release.

Closely allied to the sense of unlimited time is the feeling of space. One is so much a part of the other it is impossible to separate them. No young guide imbued as I with the romance and adventure of his work could comprehend the real meaning of time and space, but as the years went by, it penetrated my thinking, insidiously working its magic, balancing the eons against the fury of an age of technology.

As with silence, I have known this feeling in many places, but more often, perhaps, on the lakes of the far north or on the rolling tundras of the Arctic, or when looking across ranges of mountains or the open sea. Airplane travel can provide it, but a man flying high above the earth encased in a metal cocoon is so removed from naturalness, it is usually lost. In the wilderness and on the ground the old sensations are there for the simple reason that this is the way man has always known them. There is no other way, no short cuts or artificial viewpoints. A man must see it as he has always done.

It is impossible to evaluate the importance of my guiding years and their influence on me, or to draw conclusions applicable to all, just as it is futile to list everything that affected me over the years. Ask any old-timer, voyageur, trapper, or guide why he stays in the bush and his answer is usually the same: freedom to come and go, freedom of thought and action. There is an old saying that it's easier to take a man out of the bush than to take the bush out of a man, and this I believe is true.

The bush is a complex of many joys—companionship on the trail, the thrills of exploration, the impact of silence, vastness, and infinity, the good feeling of doing something for its own sake without the spur of reward, the physical satisfaction of using bodies as they were meant to be used, and moving under one's own power, the complete naturalness of living out of doors.

Guiding gave me all this, and while it began half a century ago, its influence has continued, and the truths I found there in the Quetico-Superior have been strengthened and clarified. The guides and the men with whom I traveled sensed these truths, or caught occasional glimpses of them as I did, but it took many years to make them a part of me.

I always thought that Johnny Dahl, one of my guiding companions in those early days, had a special feel for the bush, and an air that set him apart—something in his stance and the way he walked and wore his outfit. Not long ago when we were reminiscing he confirmed it.

"You know," he said, "we were a special breed of cat in those days, and felt more about that country than we ever dared let on."

He hesitated a moment, then grinned a little self-consciously and added, "We were pretty good, and a little proud of being wilderness guides."

I look at wilderness now with profound respect, knowing it must be preserved as a retreat for harried mankind in a world hurtling toward what seems to be complete divorce from the past. Knowing what it means, I can better understand the vast complex of our needs and the longing for a way of life that with many is only a memory.

Unless we keep the stream of the past
with living significance for the present,
we not only have no past but we have no present.
Tradition is not a barren pride in a dead glory;
tradition is something that provides
refreshment for the spirit.

It is something that gives us deep assurance
and a sense of destiny and a determination to
hold fast to the great things that have been done
through valor and imagination by those who
have gone before us.

FELIX FRANKFURTER

CHAPTER VI

STREAM OF
THE PAST

THERE IS NO BETTER WAY TO RECAPTURE
the spirit of an era than to follow old trails, gathering from the
earth itself the feelings and challenges of those who trod
them long ago. The landscape and way of life may be
changed, but the same winds blow on waterways, plains,
and mountains, the rains, snows, and the sun beat down,
the miles are just as long.

When I first saw the wilderness lake country, I knew
little of its past beyond the fact the logging was about over,
the great booms, rafts, and enormous mills gone. Old lumber-

jacks were still around with their stagged high-water pants and the swagger that belonged to them alone. To me that period seemed part of the time in which I lived.

Even the Indians were not entirely of the past, for some still stopped at the old campsites, fishing and traveling the lakes and rivers. Their social system and spiritual beliefs were changing, reservations had been established, areas they used to roam limited. I did not associate this with any different way of life than my own.

Absorbed in the present and involved with my own activities, I simply accepted things as they were. As a boy I had been familiar with the heroes of pioneer days, but this was a legendary period, and there was an unreality about it that had nothing to do with the present. And so it was with the meager accounts I had learned in my American-history studies of the fur trade and early settlement along the St. Lawrence River in Quebec, names like Champlain, Cartier, Radisson, and Groseilliers, and the spread of exploration toward the west were also legendary.

During my guiding in the regions the French voyageurs had traveled, I became friends with some of the halfbreed descendants of these men, and it was they who gave me my first living picture of the past. Joe Bouchard, Leo and Henry Chosa, Pierre La Ronge, and others told stories they had heard as boys of great birchbark canoes that came down the border from far-off Montreal, leaving such names to lakes, portages, and rivers as Lac la Croix, Trois-Rivières, and Maligne. Until then I had taken French names as a matter of course, but now they began to mean something.

I read Solon Buck's account of the fur trade, and of

Grand Portage, the great carrying place on Lake Superior where thousands of Indians, voyageurs, and traders gathered each summer to exchange axes, knives, and muskets for the priceless pelts of beaver—the most famous rendezvous on the continent, the halfway point of a canoe route 3,500 miles in length where brigades from Montreal met those from Fort Chipewyan, and until the early nineteenth century the most vital funnel in the trade and exploration of the northwest. From this isolated wilderness encampment, well known in the courts and banking houses of Europe, expeditions sallied forth to Rainy Lake and Lake Winnipeg, and by way of the Saskatchewan and Churchill rivers to Fort Chipewyan at the far west end of Lake Athabasca.

Grand Portage was one of the longest and most rugged portages of the entire route, nine miles of hills and swamps around the boiling rapids of the Pigeon River, a trail that tested the strength and endurance of generations of French voyageurs. Alexander Mackenzie of the Northwest Company, famed for his discoveries, described them.

"When they arrived at Grand Portage each of them has to carry eight packages of such goods and provisions as are necessary in the interior country. This is a labor which cattle cannot conveniently perform in summer as both horses and oxen were tried by the company without success.

"I have known some of them to set off with two packages of ninety pounds each and return with two others of the same weight in the course of six hours, being a distance of eighteen miles over hills and mountains." He might have added that some even carried three.

Later I read Grace Lee Nute's *The Voyageur's High-*

way, as well as the diaries of such explorers as Mackenzie, Vérendrye, and Thompson, and through them caught at last the flavor, romance, and danger of the days in which they lived. The great highway of lakes, rivers, and forests became alive, and when I paddled down waterways, ran the rapids, and made the portages those old canoemen trod, mine was a sense of personal identification so powerful at times it seemed as though I were one of them.

Their story of the two hundred years between 1650 and 1850 was a dramatic one in which fortunes in furs and supplies moved up and down the great highway. It was a time of struggle, warfare, and piracy between the rival fur companies of England, France, and the United States. A vast network of forts and posts was established throughout the north and west, and as a result, the lands were opened up, bringing settlers and development in their wake.

All this was fascinating, but it was the voyageur who captured my imagination, he who carried the tremendous loads, paddled from dawn to dark fighting waves and storms, existing on a diet of pea soup and a daily spoonful of fat. His muscle and brawn supplied the power for all the exploration and trade, but in spite of the harshness of his life, the privation, suffering, and constant threat of death by exposure, drowning, and Indian attack, he developed a nonchalance and joy in the wilderness that has never been equaled in man's conquest and exploitation of any new land. These gay French Canadian canoemen with red sashes and caps, singing in the face of monotony and disaster, were the ones who stood out.

Their contracts with the various fur companies prove profit had little to do with their choice, that it must have been something else, the lure, perhaps, of far places, the romance and adventure of a way of life they had never known before. Whatever the reason, they practically deserted the villages along the St. Lawrence for the pays d'en haute. Before embarking on any expedition, each signed an agreement, usually with a cross, for few could read or write. One to three years was the normal term of service, a bowman or steersman receiving 1,200 livres per annum, an ordinary paddler 400, and for this princely sum he agreed to do whatever was required, not to desert his master or give aid and encouragement to his rivals. A third of the wages was supplied before starting, together with his equipment, consisting of a blanket, shirt, pair of trousers, two handkerchiefs, and several pounds of twist tobacco. The penalty for desertion or insubordination enroute was flogging, or far worse, abandonment in the bush. But in spite of long absences from family and friends, grueling work on lakes and portages, they fought for the chance to go and were proud when chosen for the brigades. No worse fate could befall a young man than to be forced to remain at home.

For several years I guided with a young French Canadian, Pierre La Ronge, in whose veins ran the blood of a long line of voyageurs. From the very first he called me François, and no sooner were we together than we spoke in the patois of Old Quebec from where his people came. The longer this went on the more we acted and felt like the men from Montreal and Trois-Rivières, and after a while we felt more like voyageurs than guides of the twentieth century.

"Pierre," I might say, "when you go for catch dose trout, use hangerworm or hoppergrass."

"*Oui, oui,* François," he would reply in mock desperation, "dere ees no hangerworm or hoppergrass een dees countree. All we have eese copper spoon," and with a gesture of utter bafflement any Quebecer might envy, "What can poor Pierre do?"

When cooking the inevitable dried fruit he would announce to an invisible audience, "De prune ees de fines' berry dat grows een de swamp."

A ridiculous performance, perhaps, but it provided many laughs, and talking like men from the villages along the St. Lawrence somehow colored our attitude toward the life we were leading and gave all events, including the weather, a humorous twist.

If someone should happen to balk at the weight of a pack, invariably he would be reminded of the standard load for voyageurs, the regular 180 pounds of the two packets he had to carry, and of the great La Bonga who put them all to shame with five, a total of 450 pounds. The carrying then was done with a tumpline, a broad leather strap over the top of the head. In those early days of guiding before I had seen the kind of carrying still done by Indians and half-breeds back in the bush, I used to wonder if the old stories were true. Now I know they were, for I have seen what they can do where carrying loads is an accepted thing.

A few years ago during a packing contest, a Cree Indian carried 500 pounds. When I told of this record to some

Swampy Crees in the Hudson Bay country to the east, one of them said, "I can carry that too, and the Indian on top," and having watched him on the portages, I believed him.

The Sherpas of the Himalayas think nothing of such feats. Anthony Lovink, a companion of many Canadian expeditions, after years in this part of the world, observed; "They begin carrying as children, gradually with heavier and heavier loads, learning the art of balance, breathing, and conditioning muscles and nerves to cope with the ruggedness and rarefied atmosphere of the high mountains."

And so it must have been with the voyageurs who entered the service young. They learned by doing, and glorying in their strength, portages were a relief from paddling, a place for visiting and feeling the ground under their feet after the hazard of rapids and the waves of big lakes.

Pierre and I were no different, and when after a long paddle we finally hit the shore, we tore into the packs as though each was a personal challenge. Sometimes when the weather was foul and the trails a soggy mess, Pierre would quote from William Henry Drummond, the bard of the fur trade.

> "De win' she blow on Lac St. Claire,
>   She blow den blow some more,
>   Eef you don't drown on dees beeg lac
>   You better kip close to shore."

But the poem he loved best of all was "The Voyageur." He knew all the verses and sometimes at night when all the work was done and the time had come to crawl into our blankets, he would load up his blackened pipe, light it with a coal, get to his feet, and begin. All would go well until he came to the last verse; then his eyes grew round and dark and his voice husky as he declaimed:

"So dat's de reason I drink tonight
 To de men of de Grand Nor'Wes',
  For hees heart was young, an' hees heart was light
   So long as he's leevin' dere—
    I'm proud of de sam' blood in my vein,
     I'm a son of de Nort' Win' wance again—
      So we'll fill her up till de bottle's drain,
       An' drink to de Voyageur."

But the gaudy brigades are gone now, no longer are red-tipped paddles flashing in the sun, no more the singing and the sound of voices across the water, nothing left but crumbling forts, old foundations, and the names they left behind them. But there is something that will never be lost, the voyageur as a symbol of a way of life, the gay spirit with which he faced enormous odds, and a love of the wilderness few frontiersmen ever knew.

This is what Pierre and I thought of when we talked our broken English, and when we were together, ghosts of those days stalked the portages and phantom canoes moved down the lakes. On quiet nights it seemed we could hear the old *chansons* drifting across the water and hear their banter. I know when their story is weighed on the scales of history, the Pierres, Baptistes, and Jeans will be remembered not so much for what they did in the opening up of the continent, but for what they were. Theirs was a heritage of courage and spirit men will never forget.

Having seen most of the country within a radius of a few hundred miles of Ely, I longed to explore to the north and northwest as some of the older guides had done. Recalling their stories of the Albany, Sioux Lookout, and the Flin Flon, I knew the beautiful lake country of the Quetico-Superior was only a small part of the great route followed in the past. As years went by, it became an obsession to know the tremendous distances beyond, and to understand what motivated the voyageurs and the challenges that were theirs.

Though the country was mapped, with long-established Hudson's Bay posts scattered across it, the physical terrain was the same, with vast reaches as primitive as in the days of old.

Thus began a series of expeditions with friends who felt as I. The famous Churchill River was the first, a thousand miles or more of lakes, rapids, and waterfalls extending from Ile-à-la Crosse in Saskatchewan to Hudson Bay. Though I had known the southern fringes of the Canadian Shield, I did not realize its real meaning and continental extent. We ran all the white water we could, lined where we dared not run, fought storms on the big lakes, and came to know the bush I had dreamed about so long.

Once we followed the Camsell River north of the three-hundred-mile sweep of Great Slave Lake from the divide as far as Great Bear, with its cold, desolate barrens southwest of Coronation Gulf on the Arctic Coast. From the west end we careened down the Bear River to the Mackenzie ninety miles away, and for the first time saw the route the famous explorer had followed in his search for the Northwest Passage, only to find its mouth in the ice floes of the Arctic Ocean.

We retraced the trail of David Thompson, beginning at Reindeer Lake, 160 miles to the mouth of the Swan, and finally went down the Fond du Lac to the Hudson's Bay post at Stony Rapids on Lake Athabasca, almost 300 miles from Fort Chipewyan at its far west end. This was the starting place of the famed Athabasca brigades who each year met those from Montreal at Grand Portage some 2,000 miles away.

I saw the caribou migration on the Wolverine-Neganilini country northwest of Fort Churchill, came to know the open tundras beyond the limit of trees, and the feel of the lonely barrens along the west coast of the Bay. Like the caribou, I sought shelter in the islands of dwarf spruce known as the Taiga, the parklike stretches lying between the tundras and the treeline to the south. The land of little sticks, as it is called, Taiga is a refuge for all living things, a sanctuary from blizzards or swirling whiteness, the long night, and the eternal cold.

In 1964 we followed the Nelson, the Esquamish, and the Hayes down the historic route to Old York Factory on Hudson Bay, gazed as countless voyageurs had done over the blue and sparkling reaches of the sea itself, saw polar bears with their cubs, schools of white whales, and felt the frigid blasts from the ice pack in the straits above.

Two years later we saw the Ottawa, the Mattawa, and the French, the beginning of the route from Montreal, heard the legends of Champlain and saw the portage where he lost his precious astrolabe in 1615. We portaged dangerous rapids on the French which had claimed the lives of many voyageurs, pictured the banks with their white crosses where in the high water of spring the great canoes were all but torn apart.

We passed through the narrow dalles all diarists wrote about with fear and delight, the places where parallel, rocky ridges make narrow canal-like chutes through which the canoes speed during times of flood. We did not run them, for this was fall and the waters were low, but as we portaged beside them, we could almost hear the wild shouts as the thirty-five-foot Montreal canoes shot through, the banks close enough to touch. Then in the calm, placid area below, we looked as they had done at the broad, blue expanses of Lake Huron, with its hundreds of rocky, windswept islands and their tattered pines.

I saw the clear green headwaters of the Yukon where it flows from the height of land above Skagway down through the fabled gold fields of 1898, and its brown and sluggish flow as it passes Fort Yukon on its way to the Bering Sea.

I came to know the part the Mississippi, the Missouri, and the Yellowstone played during the fur trade, for they were also highways of the voyageurs into such rendezvous as Jackson Hole in Wyoming. There were no rivers the traders failed to explore, no matter how far or remote. Some ventured so far they never did return, but wherever they went, the goods went with them, packs that grew more valuable with every added mile from St. Louis and Montreal. The rapids cost lives, goods, and fur; every turbulent stretch of white water took its toll.

The explorers and traders spoke with dread of these disasters, the loss of men, valuable canoes and cargoes, but still they paddled on into the beaver country, penetrating farther and farther into the last unsettled lands of the continent.

Charles Grant, a Nor'wester, wrote the governor of Quebec in 1780 that "Indian trade by every communication is carried on at great expense, labour, and risk of both men and property; every year furnishes instances of the loss of men and goods by accident."

According to the Colonial Office Papers of 1786, "67 licenses were granted that year covering 163 canoes, 163 flat bottomed wooden bateaux, 2,130 men, 56,324 gallons of rum, 66,207 pounds of powder, 899½ hundred weight of ball and shot. In addition were the usual packets of ironware, kettles, beads, calico and trinkets gone up river."

Alexander Henry recorded the cargo of a typical canoe headed for the Red River country on July 20, 1800.

Merchandise 90 pounds each	— 5 bales
Canal tobacco	— 1 bale
Kettles	— 1 bale
Guns	— 1 case
Iron works	— 1 case
New twist tobacco	— 2 rolls
Leaden balls	— 2 bags
Leaden shot	— 1 bag
Sugar	— 1 keg
1 case gun powder	— 2 kegs
High wine, distilled, 9 gallons each	—10 kegs

Equipage for the voyage: Provisions for every four men to Red River, 4 bags corn, 1½ bushels in each, private property belonging to the men consisting of clothing, tobacco, etc. for themselves and families for the year, so that when all hands were embarked the canoes sunk to the gunnel.

With such factual knowledge contributed by many explorers and traders, and pieces of equipment found on portages and campsites over the years, historians became convinced that beneath many of the rapids along the Voyageur's Highway was a treasure trove of artifacts, and if it was explored with modern diving gear, they might find some of the places where accidents had occurred.

The Minnesota Historical Society, long interested in the voyageur story, organized a diving expedition to explore the Basswood River between Basswood and Crooked Lake on the Minnesota-Ontario border. This dangerous six-mile stretch had been mentioned by many early travelers and would, without question, be a good place to start.

Knowing voyageurs, like all canoemen, would run fast water wherever they could to save labor and time spent in portaging, we also knew that with their lighthearted approach to danger during the two centuries they traversed this route they must have tried many places where they should have carried, or perhaps after some regale at one of the trading posts they had thrown caution to the winds.

The first diving was done below several of the big, brawling rapids that literally boil around rocks and hidden ledges, where certain destruction would await any canoe coming down. To our surprise we found nothing, but knowing that modern canoemen never attempt such places, run only the easy ones, and that all, irrespective of the age in which they lived, are much the same, we decided after many fruitless and dangerous dives to try the relatively smooth, easy slicks of fast water instead. Even such rapids have whirlpools, treacherous currents, and hidden rocks that can mean disaster when the light is bad, the water too low, or the bowman a trifle reckless.

We concentrated on rapids they might chance, and it was then the divers found what we were looking for. I shall never forget the thrill of seeing the first emerge with a handful of rusted spear points. We ran to the shore, helped him out of the water, and took the precious iron from his hands.

"There's a lot of stuff down there," he blurted. "More where these came from."

Barely waiting to get his breath, he dove again and was joined by two others, and from then on it was a procession of trips from the bottom of the hole they had found to the shore. Soon there were piles of trade axes, spears, and leaden shot, even beads and vermilion paint, bits of broken pipes, plates, flint, steel, and copper pots.

It could well have been the disaster Alexander Henry the Younger wrote about 165 years before. In a notation of August 9, 1800, he described a typical mishap. "I perceived the canoe on the north side coming off to sault [shoot] the rapids. She had not gone many yards when by some mismanagement of the foreman, the current bore down her bow full upon the shore against a rock . . . The canoe we found flat upon the water, broken in many places . . . The loss amounted to five bales of merchandise, two bales new tobacco, one bale canal tobacco, one bale kettles, one bale balls, one bale shot, one case guns. I was surprised that a keg of sugar drifted down about half a mile below the rapids as its weight was 87 pounds; it proved but little damaged. The kegs of gun power also floated a great distance but did not leak."

I could imagine a twenty-five-foot North canoe starting down the rapids we were exploring, trying to avoid the big round boulder at its very crest. If the depth of the water was not just right, the canoe could be caught, swing broadside, ricocheting from rock to rock, swiftly filling with water as its great sides of bark and cedar were crushed, its bales sinking into the current, the voyageurs trying desperately to save what they could before scrambling for the shore to save themselves. Then the tragic aftermath, knowing the expedition might well be ended, food, weapons, clothing, blankets, and tobacco gone; ahead, starvation and possibly death.

The divers seemed incongruous in that wild setting with brilliant orange-and-black suits and sky-blue flippers. When they surfaced, coursing smoothly through the water, they were creatures of a different world against a background that had not changed since the days of the trade, the same smooth shelf of granite at the landing, the rounded boulders across the river, the swirl around the big one at the head of the rapids, and the eternal standing waves as fixed and sculptured as though they were carved from stone.

Seeing those artifacts come out of the water where they may have lain for two centuries or more was like meeting the voyageurs themselves. We laid our treasures on the rocks and looked at them with wonder. This is what they had carried and guarded with their lives; those rust-encrusted axes, those knives and spearheads had been handled last by them.

It was not until I stood again on the shore of Lake Superior at the site of old Grand Portage that the full significance and meaning came home to me. Now I could see it all—the Quetico-Superior country, Lake of the Woods and Winnipeg, Saskatchewan and the Churchill. They lay before me now—Athabasca and Great Slave, the Mackenzie and Great Bear, the Nelson and the Hayes, the St. Lawrence, Ottawa and the French, the wide expanses of lakes Huron, Michigan, and Superior, the whole broad sweep of land and water that was theirs. What I saw was a living map of lakes, rivers, and forests, of mountains and plains, a map colored with disaster and disappointment, with challenge and triumph, with hopes and dreams. It took many years to understand the voyageurs and the lives they led; seemed ages since I had guided with Pierre. I thought of him then and wondered if we would have been equal to the challenges that were theirs. I could hear him bellowing into the wind:

> "I'm proud of de sam' blood in my vein,
> I'm a son of de Nort' Win' wance again—
> So we'll fill her up till de bottle's drain
> An' drink to de Voyageur."

When I saw the name Samuel Hearne chiseled in the rock off Fort Churchill on the west coast of Hudson Bay with the date 1789 below, it meant more to me having seen the Coppermine and the Arctic Coast he finally reached.

I never see the Mackenzie River without sensing the heartbreak of the great Alexander when his dream of finding the Northwest Passage to the Orient came to naught, when after thousands of miles of travel, he found it was only another way to the Polar Sea. I can picture him looking across the endless ice floes with their fogs and constant whispering, and understand why he named one of the largest rivers on the continent "River of Disappointment."

In Montreal along the old waterfront where thousands of great canoes once embarked for the west, I think of David Thompson, the best mapmaker of them all, and how, in his old age, he was forced to sell his most precious possession to keep from starving, the theodolite he had almost lost on the Fond du Lac, the instrument which helped map more of the continent than any man had ever done.

At old Grand Portage, I like to climb to the lookout place on top of Mount Rose where Daniel Harmon used to watch the busy scene below of voyageurs packing their loads on the portage trail, the comings and goings and frantic preparations of brigades for the northwest or the east. I never see an Indian dance without thinking of John Flatt, the blind chief of the Grand Portage band, listening to the tom-toms with tears running down his weathered face as he remembered young dancers of his past, the dream dancers who may have known the last of the voyageurs. When young braves lounge around some trading post, I think of the night Chief John Graves of the Red Lake Reservation told me there was always something for them to do in the old days, hunting and fishing expeditions, gathering of wild rice and maple sugar, and the war games with distant tribes, the great feasts when they returned and how coups were rewarded and the pride of the tall young men as they boasted of their exploits.

"Today," he said, "there is nothing for them to do. They drink and get into trouble, and sometimes white men put them in jail because they do not understand. This is sad for my people and for all Indians."

History means emotion and a consciousness of what people felt as they lived in primitive ways, endured hardships, and knew triumphs. Whether it was the period before white men came, the time of the voyageurs, Spanish exploration of the Southwest, the long wagon trains along the Santa Fe or Oregon, the wilderness road of Daniel Boone or the mountain men, it is how they lived, suffered, and laughed, and what their dreams were, that determined the course of history. We can read and study, look at pictures and portrayals of those days, but the real heritage is knowing the land and those who lived upon it.

I followed the Wilderness Road of Daniel Boone across the Smoky Mountains toward the dark and bloody ground of Kentucky. The wilder reaches of those mountains look much the same as they did then, the views from grassy balds of high billowing hills, and the drifting clouds and floating mists which gave them their name. Coming by foot through Cumberland Gap for the first time and breaking out into the open meant more because of the wilderness I had known elsewhere. I could guess better the feelings of the first frontiersmen after days of climbing and hoping each ridge was the last. There in the distant blue was the unknown, hostile Indian tribes with the possibility of capture, torture, and death; I sensed their fierce joy as they thought of the land-hungry people waiting for word it was safe to move on. These men were not voyageurs in a wilderness of lakes and rivers; this was a land of dark forests and broad valleys, a land of twilight and shadows and the eternal sounds of hidden springs and rivulets.

In tracing the sun-baked trail of the Spaniard Coronado as he sought the Seven Cities of Cibola across the arid canyons and painted deserts of the Southwest, I knew what he and his men had experienced, the thirst, blowing sand, and withering heat of a land where there was no shade. From the moment the copper ball of the sun climbed above a blazing horizon until it sank trembling into the blue dusk, there was no relief. Day after day, it was the same slow plodding through hot drifting sands with a mirage before them, the glistening spires of Cibola. This was where the conquistadors faced their unknown.

In following Lewis and Clark on the upper Missouri, I marveled at the strangely sculptured cliffs and pinnacles bordering its headwaters two thousand miles from their starting point at St. Louis. I saw the Shining Mountains as they did after traversing the great plains through which the river wound toward its confluence with the Mississippi. We ran the breaks, as they called the upper rapids, portaged and lined as they had done, passed the Buffalo Jumps where Indians drove herds of the huge animals to their death on the rugged talus slopes below, we knew better than the explorers did the mountains ahead, the canyons, peaks, and passes, between them and their goal, the Pacific.

Once when the dogwood and redbud were in bloom and the ground lush with the first flowers of spring, I hiked with a group led by Justice Douglas down the old towpath trail from Cumberland at the head of the Potomac 189 miles to the tidal basin at Washington, D.C. This was the route of the famous Chesapeake and Ohio Canal built during the 1830's when the rivers were still major highways in the East. That spring I saw the river and its beauty, met its people, and skirted rapids boiling their way toward the sea, surprised a flock of great white swans resting on the waters of a quiet bend. There were tracks of deer and coons, and trees were alive with migrating birds.

We passed General Braddock's Road, built during the French and Indian Wars, crossed the far more ancient war trail of the Iroquois. The Civil War had been fought along the Potomac too, and the battlefields lay near. One day I left the towpath and hiked to Antietam, where thousands had died. It seemed strangely peaceful and unreal, but somehow I felt a little closer to those who had fought there and had seen the same trees, the flowers, the rising mists of morning.

As vital as the historic places are the people who live along the river as they have since colonial days. I visited one evening with an old couple above Fredericksburg. Dusk was settling, whippoorwills were calling, night hawks zooming overhead; no other sounds but the gurgling of water. When it grew opalescent, it seemed the scene had never changed.

"I like living here," said the old man. "Family came before the Revolution. The boys and girls moved to town, but we stayed on, Ma and me. Every so often they come back to visit, sit outside the cabin as we're doin' now, remembering when they was kids. You can still take a catfish in the river and when shad's runnin' it's almost like old times. Sometimes when the moon is full I take the old hound dog and run down a coon."

Just then we heard a baying along the ridges above the bottoms. The old man listened intently.

"That's old Major," he said. "He's on the trail of one right now."

As we sat and visited, talk of war and trouble seemed far away.

"No," he said in answer to my query, "I ain't ever goin' to move. This is where our roots are."

I rose to leave, but he begged me to stay and I followed him inside. He lit an oil lamp, touched a match to the kindling in the fireplace, then over a pitcher of apple cider we looked at an album of pictures taken during the days when the canal was still in use. As a boy he had driven a mule along the towpath, and he told me how, when rival crews from the barges would meet at the taverns along the river, there was drinking and brawling until the wee morning hours.

"I remember those days," he said. "A good time to live," and his eyes shone in the firelight.

On the Kern Plateau just below Mount Whitney in California's southern Sierras, I followed the trail of Joe Walker, the famous mountain man, who for forty years between 1821 and 1861 roamed the Southwest. It was he who discovered Yosemite and the Big Trees, and Walker Pass, the route of "manifest destiny" that led to the Mexican War.

He left his mark everywhere in the beautiful southern Sierras, and from Ardis Walker, a descendant and also a mountain man at heart, I heard the story of those adventurous days, of the rendezvous places where Old Joe met with Indians and voyageurs to exchange trade goods for fur.

As we rested our horses one day on Sherman Pass just above the little town of Kernville, we feasted our eyes on vistas of gnarled and wind-blown pines and rugged expanses to the south. I tried to imagine how it must have seemed to those who saw it first and how they felt as they looked beyond the place where we had stopped. The high country was much the same, though logging roads were creeping closer and closer and plans for its recreational development were being discussed.

"Old Joe," said Ardis, "was one of the best scouts of them all, boasted having led more successful expeditions than anyone else without ever having lost a man to Indians, starvation, or accident. Proud of belonging to his clan, feel the same about these mountains."

This was no idle statement, for Ardis, a graduate engineer, had practiced in the East until he could no longer stand the pace and had returned to his beloved Sierras to live. The blood of the old mountain man could not be denied.

With him I gained more of an understanding of those

mountains than ever before, for he loved the Kern and the plateau through which it flows, felt the area should be preserved for all time as a rendezvous for mountain men of the future.

And so it has been wherever I have gone; what I learned in the land of the voyageurs taught me what to look for everywhere, convinced me that history means the warmth of human associations, that while great events may find their place in books and museums, it is the people themselves who really counted. No longer did a country provide only opportunities for fishing, hunting, and camping places. I had found something more important. When one followed the trails of the past, no matter who the legendary figures were, voyageurs, conquistadors, or gold seekers, somehow their feelings came through, and when they did, the land glowed with warmth and light.

In the beginning God created
the heaven and the earth.
And the earth was without form and void;
And darkness was upon the face of the deep.
And the spirit of God moved upon the
face of the waters.

GENESIS

CHAPTER VII

FACE OF
THE EARTH

THE EXPERIENCES OF MY YOUNG MANHOOD
gave me some understanding of the meaning of wilderness,
and my identification with its historic background, a

sense of belonging to both past and present, increased, but I still did not have the whole picture, a feel of the terrain itself.

Mountains had once reared mighty snow-clad peaks in the Quetico-Superior, the arms of ancient seas washing almost to their bases. Erosion had leveled them to a broad plateau, while volcanic eruptions had forced lavas to the surface, breaking the basic formations still more, twisting and contorting them, penetrating the bed rock to the point where it is hard to know the old from the new. After many millions of years, the ice age had come with huge continental glaciers grinding and leveling the roots of the Laurentian mountains, polishing and gouging them until almost nothing remained of the great highlands.

In all this mass of factual information an element was missing, and for years I did not know what it was. While I was a student in geology at the University of Wisconsin, something happened that gave me a clue, a minor incident perhaps, but the sort of experience which often sets in motion a train of clarifying ideas. In a mineralogy class we had been studying crystals, their formation and detailed structure, angles of facets and how they were the same no matter what the background matrix, temperature, pressure, or cause of crystallization. For weeks we had lived with formulae and measurements, indices of light refraction and how to distinguish hexagons from tetrahedrals, but instead of being fascinating, it had grown increasingly boring, no different, I thought, from memorizing lists of historical dates without knowing the problems and cultural backgrounds of the peoples involved. One day Dr. N. H. Winchell, noting my impatience, came over to me.

"I've decided," I said, "to drop mineralogy. I like living things. All this is dead," and I pushed my tray of specimens to one side.

"Listen," he said. "These crystals are alive, their atoms constantly moving, each one a world and a universe in itself. There is nothing dead except in your own mind."

Shocked, I went back to work while his words pounded their way into my consciousness—"crystals alive . . . moving . . . each one a world in itself"—and from that moment the science of mineralogy became a living thing; never again was I to look at a rock or a crystal without remembering.

Dr. C. K. Leith, head of the geology department, told us we should not look at the earth as a static thing, that it is fluid and viscous, with continents rising and sinking, mountains forming as in the past, even the great seas stirring in their beds, changing position and volume. Through his eyes we saw the shaping of the earth over untold millions of years with nothing ever permanent or at rest, the entire planet as alive as the crystals themselves. Time, he told us, was the great illusion, and if we could see the earth with the perspective of eons instead of years, we would understand.

Life—movement—constantly evolving earth processes—this was an exciting concept, a way of looking at the world I had never envisioned before, the basis for a sense of terrain, a feeling for the face of the earth and the forces that were molding it. Here was the clue I had missed.

This was even more meaningful during the summer I spent with the Geological Survey in northern Wisconsin. In preparation that spring, members of the crew were given several monographs to read, and no sooner had I begun delving into the huge, dusty tomes than they too became alive. Those old reports were more than textbooks, they were living records of years of fieldwork with photographs, maps, and profiles of the physical features of the land, something I could now begin to appreciate. Not until we were in camp in the headwaters country of the St. Croix River did the full realization come.

Assigned to one of the geologists as a compassman, my duty was to run lines and pace off chains and rods accurately enough to keep our maps aligned with parallel surveys. Iron exploration was part of the work, and I learned to watch the gyrations of a magnetic dip needle and interpret what they meant. So conscious did we become of what lay beneath the surface, so involved with what the needle showed, we could almost picture the formations of limonite or bog ore lying sometimes a hundred feet beneath the great blanket of sand, gravel, and rock known as glacial moraine. Where the layer was deep, the needle barely quivered, but where it was shallow, the magnetic attraction was so powerful it fairly danced. Surface outcrops were more exciting still, for there we recorded the angles of intrusive veins of quartz, granite, and basalt for possible indications of other more valuable metals such as gold, silver, and copper. We took samples of all formations, and by the end of a day our packs were heavy.

This was the lure of prospecting, the lure of the mother lode, some concentrated deposit to which all indications invariably lead. No mineralized ledges were ever neglected, for though the area had been thoroughly combed for metals long before, there was still a chance of finding some place that in the furor of going into a raw and unexplored wilderness for the first time had been overlooked. Massive batholiths of granite and basalt indicated contact zones where minerals were often richer than anywhere else. Sedimentary layers of stratified and cemented sand and pebbles spoke of rivers and shores of ancient seas, and when there were slates and shales, we thought of the great swamps of the carboniferous era with possible beds of coal.

I learned the difference between the eras of the Cambrian and Precambrian, the significance of the dividing line between the age of animal forms in the lower paleozoic era and the eons reaching backward to the very beginnings when there was little evidence of any life. One day I found my first fossils, trilobites embedded distinctly in an ancient formation of solidified ocean silt, and in that moment I plunged backward a billion years. We worked along studying the outcrops, watching the dip needle, looking at the broad configuration of the land until within me was a growing awareness of the vast changes that had taken place over an infinity of time.

During that summer we surveyed roads and trails, plotted them on relief maps, made a study of the Yellow River from its spring-fed source to its lower reaches where it runs into the St. Croix. We measured depth and flow, bottom structure, ledges, rapids, and tributaries. Wading rivers and creeks was not new to me, but this had little to do with rising trout or the sound of whitethroats at dusk. What I discovered on the Yellow was the physical character of a waterway, and through this a new comprehension of all streams and an intimate involvement with their real nature.

So engrossed did I become that season with my new-found knowledge and the young geologists with whom I worked, that it was only natural to believe that this was the life for me. No other field could possibly be so rewarding as exploring for minerals, and I would be free to spend the rest of my life in the wilds.

I never quite forgot that dream, and after graduating in agriculture, kept it alive by teaching a course in geology, but there were times in the classroom when the vision of being a field geologist haunted me, and before my first year was over, I knew I must find out if this were what I really wanted to do. The only solution was to return to college for more work in geology. While reluctant to leave the Mesabi Range and the woods I had roamed, I took the drastic step and returned to the university. By preparing myself for a new career, I would then move back into the north.

The first few months went well, the cabin on Kennedy

and the country I had come to know were almost forgotten. There were times, however, when it seemed I could stand the separation no longer, and with growing dismay I noted other signs, especially on field trips when I would break away from the group to find some vantage point where I could be alone. At such times I would picture the glacial ice fields with their rivers roaring out of the north, carrying with them the debris of half a continent. On the high hills and ledges above Baraboo I could see it better than anywhere else, and it brought back my constant need of more than geology itself, something beyond the accumulation of knowledge.

Back in the department I would be reasonably content for a while, then without warning those disturbing visions came again, lakes with the sting of wind in my face, camps at dusk with the calling of the loons, sunsets with spruces etched against them, dawns with mists rising out of the bays. Such memories could not be stilled, and I treasured them until at times my hunger seemed more than I could bear.

In spite of my love for geology, I began to wonder if making it a working profession was the solution after all. The reasons for surveys, prospecting, and exploration for minerals became increasingly clear. Success was employment by some mining company, and the real problems, after discovery, would be access, extraction of metals from crude ore, even marketing and distribution of the final product. This was mining engineering with the practical goal of industrial use, geology the knowledge that made it possible. While vital to the country's economy, geology to me was a way of understanding the land itself, the key to values not to be processed or sold. With this point of view there could be no middle ground, so I left the university once more and headed north to the only kind of prospecting I would ever do.

After that experience the Quetico-Superior took on a new dimension. True, its lakes still sparkled in the sun while the rapids sang their old delightful song, but the granites, gneisses, and schists intruding the Canadian Shield had more significance. Glaciation too seemed more like an open book, the ice-polished surfaces with their striations indicating the way the glaciers had come. Participating in an aerial glaciological survey with Dr. Wallace Atwood, a great geographer who had spent his life studying the shape of the land in many parts of the world, and seeing the Quetico-Superior through his eyes finally gave me the last dramatic chapter in its evolution.

As with others who had extended my vision, it was he who made knowing important. Each man was more than a specialist in his field, and whether the field was crystallography, the broad brush of earth-shaping forces, or glaciology, within each was a deep, almost philosophical involvement with man and his environment that transcended practicality. Winchell, the mineralogist, had shown me the unseen world of atoms, while Leith, with his understanding of volcanology and continent-shaping, made the entire planet a living thing. Now with Atwood I saw the glaciers of the ice age for the first time and learned the part they had played in carving the eroded Laurentians into what they are today. These men gave me the knowledge and scope to interpret anew the face of the land.

One day as we were flying high above the stippled blue and green of the border country, Dr. Atwood pictured the scene at the end of the Cambrian almost a billion years ago—the high mountains that came from the folding of rock masses thousands of feet in thickness, snowy peaks with wide valleys between them, eons of rain and snow, of cold and heat breaking them up and wearing them down to a broad tableland, rivers carrying off the debris to the south, the grand outwash plains forming sandstones, slates, and conglomerates in seas washing the bases of the ranges.

Then he described the vast intrusions of lava boiling up through the old formations, black basalts, granites, and crystalline fingers of white quartz, until the roots of those ancient mountains were all but lost in the confusion. The weathering and erosion continued with new rivers flowing to the south until where the high Laurentians stood, the land was almost flat, a rugged peneplain of twisted and tortured rock.

He laid the stage for the last million years and for the four great ages of glaciation that had covered half the continent, ice masses two miles in thickness moving slowly down the north, smoothing the bed rock, pushing ahead and carrying mountainous masses of topsoil, gravel, and boulders, which it spread over the land, disrupting drainages until there was a veritable tangle of new watercourses flowing in all directions. All life was destroyed in its path, and when the ice was gone, the surface lay bleak and frozen, a desert of the north.

The rock was gouged, he explained, as though it were putty, the glaciers moving over it like many-fingered lathes digging lake beds and channels out of the rock hundreds of feet in depth. They continued in motion for hundreds of thousands of years. Even toward the end of the glacial periods when the ice fronts were melting and retreating, the great masses were moving forward, like rock-shod rasps scraping off soil from the bedrock, dumping the richness of millions of years of erosion and decay on the northern tier of states.

The picture he described lay before us as our plane flew high above it, a series of narrow, parallel lakes pointing toward the southwest, and I could see the glacier like a clawed hand shaping the face of the land. That day the picture of the country was vividly clear, the smooth ledges of granite along the shores, the foaming white lace of rapids, the portages beside them or across morainic dams, the vast complex of waters that once had run serenely to the sea. It was as though I were a boy again, making dams in spring rivulets beside the road, playing God with a stick in my hands, forcing the water to run in every direction but where it wanted to go. The same thing had happened here with huge deposits of moraine spilled over the old established patterns of river systems. I saw the land as it must have been after the glacier's retreat, the slow seepage of waters through sand and gravel, its gradual arrangement as it sought its level, its impoundment between ridges where there was no escape, the quaking bogs of spruce, tamarack, and heather of today.

As we flew over Saganaga Lake with its picturesque islands, Dr. Atwood spoke again. "Those islands," he said, "are the tops of rock formations so hard even the ice could not grind many of them down—all that is left of volcanic cores." Then his face lit up with expectation. "The striations should be good there. If the ice could not level those knobs, it must have marked them deeply."

We circled low enough to see their rounded crests and the stand of trees that had taken root, the tops so evenly shaped it looked as though a gigantic shears had trimmed them into a symmetrical crown of green.

"Little soil there," he continued. "Possibly six inches or a foot since the ice left ten thousand years ago."

I remembered a fire sweeping over such an island during a long drought when the shallow layer of humus was dry as dust. In half an hour the trees were gone, the shrubs and flowers, the mosses and lichens—a few minutes to undo the work of a hundred centuries.

A year later when the island lay white and bare, washed clean by a season's rains and snows, I paddled by. It was hard to believe what had happened to the covering of trees that had taken so long to mature. A fragile wilderness—I shall never forget it.

When that survey ended, I felt enriched far beyond what we had actually done. Lakes and rivers extended far into the

Canadian north; ice had covered it all with the identical pattern of winding eskers, tumbled masses of moraine, parallel lakes and smooth faces of rock. Whether along the Churchill or the Athabasca, Great Slave, or Hudson Bay, the story was no different.

One day on the shores of Great Bear Lake in the land of "little sticks," I found dogwood, linnaea, and fireweed growing in profusion. It was like meeting old friends, and on the hills and tundras, I found more, the cold dwarfed heathers, birches, and willows. Almost stemless in that frigid clime, they lay nearly flat against the ground, but the leaves and flowers, though miniature, were the same as those to the south. I need never feel strange again, no matter how far from home.

In Alaska I finally saw vast living glaciers such as the Malaspina with its forty-mile front to Yakutat and the sea, the blue-green fjords of Glacier Bay with winding tongues of ice coming out of their throats, their booming fronts as bergs broke off and crashed into the waters below. Not until I saw the ice cap over the St. Elias Range, with black and jagged peaks of mountains showing through, did I know what the north must have looked like long ago. Those gleaming fields of blue and white, the freshly scarred surfaces of rock, the impact of flowing ice on everything in its path closed the cycle and gave me the continental sweep I needed, the sense of millennia and an understanding of what had taken place during the million-odd years of glacial advances and retreats.

There was more, however, to the shaping of the land than

glaciation, an older and more violent force of fire and flames and convulsions of the earth's crust that had formed the continents and their mountains millions of years before the coming of the ice.

In the Katmai region of Alaska I first caught the feeling of the subterranean forces producing volcanoes and earthquakes, thrusting lavas from the earth's molten interior toward the surface and spewing hot cinders and gases over vast areas. You can read of such events and see pictures of them, but they mean little until you actually come in contact with the forces themselves, see them in action, smell the fumes and gases, and walk the ground above them. Only then can their power be felt.

In the Valley of Ten Thousand Smokes, I saw fumeroles for the first time, the funnels, cracks, and passageways carrying gases from the molten interior of what a short time ago was an active volcano. Half a century before an eruption had taken place that covered a hundred miles around. On one unforgettable day when one of the old cones, Mount Trident, was showing activity, with yellow sulfurous fumes swirling high above it, I heard rumbling deep in the earth and knew what a coming cataclysm could mean if the forces were again unleashed, forces which had been sculpturing the land for uncounted millions of years, and could begin again.

A silt-laden river was carving the colored beds of ash in the valley, working its way down toward the bedrock, and I wondered if it would complete its work before it had to start anew. I thought of the little Indian village of Savanovski down the river and of a gray and weathered wooden cross I had found leaning against a tangle of grass and willows, all that was left at the site of the Russian church. The area was completely covered with ash and grown over with sedges, the people long forgotten, brown bears wading the shallows of the winding, braided stream in their never ending search for red salmon coming up from the sea.

At Anchorage after the last earthquake, I looked at the destruction that had shaken the city on its foundations and the bed of glacial clay high above Cook Inlet where homes slid into the sea. I flew over Seward and saw how the tidal wave had smashed the waterfront and completed the horrors of the quake itself, stark evidence of the instability of all areas along the continental rim of fire and of the forces underneath which could destroy all the works of man.

Before me are three stones, one a smoothly polished piece of Knife Lake slate from the erosion of the Laurentians. Dark gray in color, this specimen came from the deposition of clays and their final hardening after erosion; across its surface many scratches, the marks of stones once held in the ice.

The second is a bit of pumice from Katmai's volcanic valley, orange and Chinese red with dark crystalline inclusions. It came from deep within the earth, once part of a gaseous explosion from inside the cone of an active volcano. Porous, and light enough to float, I found it among ten thousand others washed up on a beach at the mouth of the Brooks River where it enters Naknek Lake.

Fishermen fly in from the old army base at King Salmon to a little resort there, but seldom go the eighteen miles by jeep to see the volcanic area. Salmon, rainbows, and Dolly Vardens are more important than the desolation below Mount Trident. One night I listened to their stories while the neon-lighted juke box played rock-and-roll and the sun painted the tops of the mountains with brilliant colors. The brown tusk of a mammoth stood in one corner of the lodge; taller than a man, and perfectly preserved by the frozen muck in which it lay, it was found by one of the workmen while digging a trench for a sewer. That creature lived between the ice ages, possibly long before men discovered their way over the Siberian land bridge from the mainland of Asia.

The third specimen is a wave-washed pebble of greenstone, one of the oldest rocks on earth. It came from a formation that lies close to the surface in the Quetico-Superior and in many places of the Canadian Shield. Geologists are not sure of its origin, but all agree it could have been the metamorphosed original crust of the earth after its cooling, going back three or four billion years. Through it is a delicate filigree of quartz which, during some period of volcanic action, forced its gaseous way through the crevices. But more intriguing to me are two rounded holes on its surface, each of them three quarters of an inch in diameter and half an inch in depth. They are as perfectly round as though made with a drill, one on the flat top surface, the other at its edge.

Sometime during its history this stone lay in a riverbed held in a vise by larger rocks. A grain of quartz was trapped above it, settled on its surface where a slight roughening held it momentarily, but long enough for the churning waters to move it in a circular orbit, roughening still further the spot where it began. Round and round it went for many years until the hole was smooth and deep. Probably during some violent freshet in the spring the big boulders moved and the pebble shifted position until it was caught in a vise once more, this time with its edge uppermost. Again a grain of quartz began to work, always the tiny circle, always and forever the slow, whirling motion until another hole was formed like the first.

Once more the riverbed shifted, and the pebble with the two round holes was spewed from its bed to be caught by the ice and carried far to the south in a mass of glacial moraine that ended in the cold waters of what is now Lake Superior. It was there I found it on a beach. Though I examined hundreds of all shapes and sizes, this was the only one with rounded holes. But this is not the end of the story, for long after I am gone it will lie somewhere nearby. It has no use, so will not be crushed or changed except by the elements; its story will go on as before, and perhaps in some new river born of another ice age, a third hole will be drilled along the other edge.

I look at these stones, study them, know their names, how they were formed and where they have been, just as I know the names of flowers, birds, and trees, and the part they play in the life of the region. One lifetime is far too short to know all the answers to any environment; what I have learned is only an infinitesimal part of the story. Even so, I have gained a sense of wholeness I did not have before. My prospecting would go on and on, looking for the mother lodes at the headwaters of forgotten creeks, the sources of treasures which mean more to me than gold or precious stones.

*Only a mountain has lived long enough
to listen objectively to
the howl of a wolf.*

ALDO LEOPOLD

CHAPTER VIII

A MOUNTAIN
LISTENS

T HE HOWL OF A WOLF IN THE NORTH MEANS
wilderness. It is the background music of a great symphony
of sound coming from a multiplicity of living things upon
which it depends. The wolf is a creature of beauty, significance, and power, occupying the very peak of an ecological
structure built of infinite relationships.

The broad base of this pyramid of life includes the creatures of humus, a microcommunity of soil organisms in a vast

composite of decay with its bacteria, viruses, and molds, its worms, larvae, and hosts of crawling things that prepare the way for larger forms, the moles and shrews who in their burrowing, aerate the humus and permit the trickling waters to flow through. Next are fungi, lichens, mosses, ferns, and the smaller rodents such as mice and squirrels, and with them the birds who live on seeds, and insects of flowers, grasses, shrubs and trees.

As the pyramid narrows, other forms appear, the rabbits, foxes, cats and bears, grouse, waterfowl, hawks and owls, and at last, near the very top, such great browsing creatures as deer, caribou, and moose. I like to think that at the very tip of this interdependent complex stands the timber wolf, majestic and alone, the result of millennia of evolutional changes and adaptations to its habitat, and to all forms of life composing it. This is the world of ecology, a subject so vast no mind as yet has ever fathomed its secrets. As John H. Storer says, "Many of them can probably never be unraveled, but the basic principles are known, and on the functioning of these known principles depends the future of all human lives."

Long before I entered this mysterious world, I was intrigued with the wolf as a symbol of wildness. I admired it for its beauty and strength and what it meant in the north, the impact of its bloodlines when crossed with native dogs in the breeding of huskies for use on the trails. Resembling a police dog with much the same stature and coloring, the body is brownish-gray, sprinkled with black and brown, with darker tones over the head and through the magnificent flaring ruff of the shoulders. Sometimes it is almost black, and in the far Arctic may be as creamy-white as a polar bear.

One of the largest predators on the continent, it ranges in weight from 65 to 150 pounds, can be six feet or more from nose to the tip of the tail, and two to three feet high at the shoulder. Together with the coyote, which is much smaller and less startlingly colored, it once occupied some seven million square miles of the continent and was numbered by hundreds of thousands. Today the wolf is rare in the United States; possibly no more than 500 all told, and nearly all within the confines of the Quetico-Superior.

While many creatures can live close to the habitations and works of man, the wolf is truly an animal of the wilds. Loons epitomize the waterways of the north, but they can breed and survive on lakes rimmed by summer cottages and disturbed by motorboats. The pileated woodpecker, the largest of its breed next to the ivory-billed, depends on the grubs and insects of old trees found originally in virgin forests. Now these trees are hard to find except in such reservations as parks or forests, or along residential avenues.

Deer are not repelled by towns or farms, but feed along fringes of open meadows and garden plots. Even moose graze the bogs around the oil rigs of the Kenai. But wolves are a different breed, and like the caribou, will not thrive for long where their range is too closely circumscribed by roads or mechanization. When the howl of one is heard, it always means the old terrain.

I crossed a lake the other day on skis, the ice thick and covered with deep snow. There were deer tracks along the shores, and I could see the browse line where they had fed on the cedars as far up as they could reach. They stayed close to their food, and the open reaches were smooth and unbroken. This was the north in February, silent and unperturbed, the only sound the hiss of my skis on the brittle crust. In passing through a narrows, I noticed the track of a wolf. It was broad as my hand, came straight across the ice toward the shore where the deer had been feeding.

That night I was thrilled to hear one call. Different from the high, varied medley of a coyote, the howl of a timber wolf is full-throated and deep, more of a bawl than a cry. As I listened, I thought of the huskies around the Indian and Eskimo villages in the far north, and how under a full moon or where the aurora was blazing across the horizons, new tones came in, until the dogs seemed to sing with a haunting harmony that carried with it all the cold and barren loneliness of the Arctic.

Yellowstone Kelly, a famous scout of the old West, once described the howling of both wolves and dogs.

"It is in stormy weather that the wolf appears to be in his element, the unearthly chorus ranging all the changes of the gamut startles the hunter in camp or the traveler by night. A wolf delights in getting on some point or rock in a storm and howling in unison with the blast that sweeps through the gulches and canyons of the foothills. The wild dogs that infest Indian camps howl in chorus like the wolves, and it requires an expert to distinguish between the two."

This was written almost a century ago, and it is good to think that even today it is possible to hear the "unearthly chorus." When Aldo Leopold said, "Only a mountain has lived long enough to listen objectively to the howl of a wolf," he meant that man, in his engrossment with conquering the wilds and eliminating from it all animals interfering with his needs, listens through ancient fears colored by legends of bloodthirsty, ravening beasts, killing wantonly and even threatening man himself.

The story of Red Riding Hood paints the wolf as it has been done for centuries, and modern man, in spite of his knowledge, has changed little in his attitude since pagan times when the old ones told their misty tales to the young. Those who have studied the part this great animal plays in the ecology of the land know how intimately it is involved with all the creatures of its environment, and how tenuous is its position of power. But even those who have dedicated their lives to unraveling this maze seldom live long enough to guess the wolf's true meaning or fully appreciate Leopold's observation.

My first interest in the wolf, during the early years in the Quetico-Superior, was not ecological; and though I knew the basic principles, I had not as yet grasped its broad significance as related to predation and the effect over a long period of time on herds of deer, moose, and caribou. Whenever I heard or saw one, it was the highlight of a trip.

On Kennedy Lake, I watched a pack feeding on the carcass of a buck not a quarter of a mile from the cabin. I had no glasses so contented myself with a pageant that to me, not knowing, was one of horror and revulsion. What it meant, or the place the wolf occupied in the overall picture, I did not realize. But in spite of predation, I liked wolves, watched and trailed them in the wintertime and during the spring and summer located their dens. I talked to Indians, trappers, hunters, and game wardens who, almost without exception, were convinced that all such varmints as bears, mountain lions, and wolves should be hunted and killed.

Once I saw a kill being made. It was during my first years of guiding, and while I have long forgotten any details of that trip, the experience is as vivid as the day it happened. We were paddling down the Basswood River on our way to Crooked Lake when I saw a deer running leisurely along a barren, rocky slope paralleling the river. To my surprise, a wolf moved slowly behind, keeping a distance of some thirty yards from its prey. It seemed to move without effort, drifting along like a shadow. Fascinated, it never occurred to us to shout or distract its attention. We stopped paddling, frozen for the moment by the scene before us.

Then the wolf dashed forward, closed the gap, and with a movement as in slow motion, caught the deer by its nose. The stricken animal turned a somersault and struck the ledge, breaking its neck. Instantly the wolf was upon it and the struggle was over. Only then did it see the canoe; it stood motionless for an instant, threw up its head, and bounded back into the spruces. We turned toward shore, jumped into the shallows, and ran up the slope to the dead animal, bled it and cut off a haunch of venison for supper. Even though the doe was old, it would be a welcome change from fish and bacon. The wolf circled around warily; we could hear it in the brush, and once caught a glimpse.

Later I learned that wolves prey mostly on the old and very young, and those crippled or diseased, and while the premise has been challenged, and there are exceptions, I believe that generally it is true, and the animals caught are those not quite as swift and aware. As a result, over a long period of time the survivors are stronger, more virile and alert because of the elimination of breeding stock that inevitably could mean degeneration or even extinction. I know now wolves are as much a part of the ecological picture as a hawk feeding on mice, a pike on minnows, or a squirrel burying cones, that they have pruned the herds of game for thousands of years and that the pruning has had the same beneficial effect as when a fruit tree is trimmed of its dead, infected, or unnecessary branches.

Wolves continued to intrigue me, and I tracked them across timbered ridges and valleys, found that hunting trails were often a hundred miles or more in length, great elliptical circles taking several weeks to cover, always crossing in certain places and keeping the same general direction, depending on depth of snow or the presence of game. Frozen lakes and streams were their highways, and kills made by driving game from the shelter of brush and trees onto the ice. Often traveling along ledges relatively free of drifted snow, they rested on high promontories where nothing would escape their attention. From such positions the leaders called the members of a pack. Whenever I found the round, oval bed of one, I would rest there and survey the terrain as through the eyes of a hunting wolf.

Charley Laney, a Finnish trapper, told me more of their

hunting trails. One day as we followed his trap line, we came to a narrow defile between two rocky formations. There in a snare was a huge wolf, almost black over its ruff, and yellowish-white underneath, a color phase rare in this part of the country.

"A good place," he told me, as he unfastened the wire snare and reset it. "Get one here every three weeks. Always cross in the same place."

From there we traveled in the general direction of the hunting route, being careful never to get too close for fear the animals would catch our scent and change their habits. The next snare was where the route led over a narrow peninsula jutting out into a lake. They used this as a shortcut, rather than the long way around its tip. I noticed moose and deer had followed it too.

"Two years ago, I got several here," said Charley, "but guess they've gotten wise."

He unfastened the snare, set it in a different place where the trail went between two boulders with just enough room to pass.

"Should be a good one," he said, admiring his work and brushing the snow with a spruce branch to cover our tracks. "They'll be back and we'll get one if a deer doesn't stumble into it."

On that trip we covered many miles along the great hunting trail, going almost due north, until it disappeared on the white expanses of Knife Lake heading toward the Quetico.

"Don't know how far them critters go," said Charley,

looking across the lake, "but wherever it is, they'll be back. They always come around."

I came to know many woodsmen who had spent a lifetime in the bush, and found all agreed that once a route was known, snaring or trapping was relatively simple because of old established crossings. They had stories to tell of personal encounters with wolves, some accurate up to a point, all embroidered with vivid imaginings. Laney was no exception, and one night when we stayed in a little log shack he had built, he told me the harrowing story of a trapper the wolves had attacked, and how, in exhaustion and at last crawling on hands and knees through the snow, he had reached his cabin, kicked open the door, and with his last strength, slammed it in their teeth.

"Close," he said, "too close for comfort. Can see them devils snarlin' and snappin' just afore he made it."

Jack Linklater, son of a Scotch factor of a Hudson's Bay post and a Cree woman and one of the finest woodsmen I have ever known, felt different.

"In all my life," he told me one night, "I've never known of a single instance where a wolf has killed a man. One whiff of our scent and they're gone."

The huskies of our dog team stirred and tugged at their chains. For some reason they were restless.

"The dogs know when they're around," Jack said, looking at the spring moon. "They're close tonight. With all that wolf blood in 'em they can't forget."

Jack told me the usual pack was a family group of four or five, that in their hunting, they would not only follow deer, their major source of food, but would cover the edges of swamps and bogs, alder-grown margins alive with mice and rabbits, and eat anything, including berries, fruit, and fish.

Skirting a marsh one day, I found that several had hunted together, knowing if a rabbit was startled, one of the others might catch it. I learned that wolves could hunt like foxes and coyotes, standing quietly in the grassy jungle of some meadow, listening for the slightest sound, then pounce with all four feet bunched tightly together. On a windy afternoon with the breeze in my favor, I watched one for half an hour before I was discovered, and though I could not see what luck the wolf had, it made several pounces and no doubt caught enough mice to stifle its hunger while waiting for larger game.

I found out the animals stayed close together on ridges, but spread out in open valleys to better cover their range. There were signs of high intelligence in their hunting, evidence of ambush and relays, and that in pursuit they often ran in single file to conserve energy in breaking a trail through heavy snow.

Tom Denley, a ranger with the U.S. Forest Service, told me of an instance where a wolf lay on a windfall beside a deer trail.

"I didn't see the kill," said Tom, "but found the imprint of a wolf's body on the windfall and what was left of the carcass down below. More important, another wolf had followed the deer and driven it to the ambush."

He agreed with Jack Linklater that most of the packs

were small, five to seven animals, but told me he had once seen the tracks of a mighty gathering of twenty-two on Crooked Lake, no doubt the joining of several family groups.

One summer I discovered where a pair had denned, and through my glasses, watched the coming and going of the adults, then later the vigilance and solicitude with which they guarded the pups, the feeding, training, and long hours of play, until the eventual moving away in the fall. It became increasingly hard to believe the stories of ferocity as I observed them basking in the sunlight on their gravel hillside, playing together as puppies.

The following winter I skied into the Thomas-Frazer area with a state game warden, Urho Salminen. As a member of the state's predator-control program, he was running a line, using a far more deadly poison than strychnine, the newly discovered potassium cyanide. Weeks before, he had scattered the pellets on lakes the wolves would cross, or where there were kills lying on the ice. This was merely a routine trip to pick up the carcasses, skin them out, and replenish the poison, but it revealed to me what poisoning could do, not only to wolves, but to all other predators. At the time, reduction and possible elimination was considered a necessary part of game management. Practiced widely in the West, it had resulted in near extinction over huge areas. Now it had come to the Quetico-Superior.

The amazing thing to me was the efficiency of the poison. We often found the bodies of several wolves, foxes, and coyotes at one station, some frozen stiff and still standing in the snow, so swift was the reaction of the cyanide. Eagles, ravens, and jays were around, and the tracks of weasels and mink. No one knew how many lesser forms were involved, but I began to see that if the program continued, all wildlife in the area would suffer, and I wondered if the price of control was too high.

During the years following wolf trails and listening to their songs at night, I realized, as one always does when knowledge finally takes the place of bias and misconception, that more important than observation was to learn the relationship of the species to all other forms of life, and to the terrain itself.

My interest inevitably involved me in an ecological point of view, and as time went on there were vague intimations of the truth that any change, no matter how minute, could upset the balance of the whole.

One summer I had the good fortune to spend several months with a scientific expedition studying the Quetico-Superior and its various creatures in relation to their habitat. It was then I first caught the meaning of ecology as a concept, and as I look back, one thing stands out, its impact as a basic understanding. More than knowledge, it was deeply involved with my own attitude and emotional reaction to the wilderness. A visceral sort of thing beyond mind and factual information, it was an inherent feeling that went down into that vast primordial well of consciousness, the source of man's original sense of oneness with all creation, a perspective reinforced with logic and reason, cause and effect, and scientific method.

Here was an ancient background shaped by eons of ad-

justment to climate, soil, and water, and by all living things
to each other. This was the true story of evolution, not only
an awareness of the intricate ways in which it came about,
but an understanding of the pyramid itself, and from this
vantage point came a sense of wholeness and completion.

To enumerate all the experiences of that memorable
summer and how they contributed to my grasp of ecology in
a book describing the major open horizons of my life would
be impossible. There were a few, however, I remember
vividly, such as the time we paddled by a great stand of
red and white pine, then decided to land and look it over
from a high hill. I had seen such trees before, but that day
I saw them for the first time. We beached the canoes, walked
inland, and climbed the ridge. The entire forest lay below
us, pines up to three hundred years of age, with trunks as
tall and straight as masts; the reds were rosy brown, the
whites, black. No underbrush grew beneath them, the floor
deep with needles and duff.

One of the scientists explained that this was the ultimate and final stage of succession and growth, all other surrounding types merely paving the way. He pointed out a
neighboring growth of aspen and birch which had followed
a fire or wind storm, and another somewhat older, mixed
with balsam and young pines, showing their tops among
them. In half a century or more all such stands would mature and die, giving the pines the chance they had been
waiting for.

A mosaic of habitats, each was associated with a charac-
teristic community of plants and animals influenced by the

variables of altitude, temperature, sunshine and wind, rain-
fall, drainage, and humidity, and finally the physical character of the land itself. No two were exactly alike, though
there seemed to be a basic core of similarity that gave it a
certain consistency and stability. The pines were only part of
the total picture.

This was the case in every component of the mosaic
whether forest, bog, or granite ridge, a constant changing
from pioneer growths to some final form. Each stage had its
own biotic structure, beginning always with the microforms
that prepared the soil for what was to come, contributing in
unknown and mysterious ways to the nutrient needs of all.

In Europe, one of the men explained, foresters found it
unwise to replant pines immediately after logging. It was
better to follow nature's way of replenishment by allowing
natural successions to run through their ancient cycles of
growth and decay.

We sat there looking over the sea of pine tops, the soft,
feathery expanses of the whites, the stiff angular branches of
the reds. Some of the older white pines were flattening at
the top, proof of advanced age.

"You can get a faster crop by planting pines after fire or
logging," continued the forester, "but the trees will not be as
straight or tall as these." Sometimes man cannot wait, for-
getting there are no shortcuts in nature.

That day I could not help but think of the wolf and how
he too was part of the long successions. Where we rested was
no doubt one of their lookout points. A mature forest would
have no game, but the aspen and birch would be worth
hunting. The forest would have no deer, and if all the trees

were full-grown over a great area, wolves would decrease in numbers and be toppled from their throne. A bolt of lightning or a campfire left untended could change it overnight.

In the distance lay a round glacial bog, a good hunting area; in the grasses around it were mice, voles, and rabbits. A marsh hawk sailed slowly across it, circled, and returned, wings barely moving as it coasted the wind. This too was changing, and even from where we sat I could see how the spruce and tamarack had taken root on the hummocks of sphagnum and heather, pioneers that spelled the death of the swale, for eventually the forest would grow into and over it, the mosses and grasses die, and all life dependent on it change, the marsh wren, weasels, and foxes, the lynx, and even wolves. While such areas often continued for many centuries, to man's short point of view, it seemed endless, for there was never stability for long, only a continual rearranging of all living forms. We could guess what would happen, but could not see its end.

Some time later at the edge of the bog I caught a red-backed mouse. Confused and frightened, it had no place to hide, for in my stumbling I had no doubt destroyed its runways. Its back was rusty-brown, underside gray, the tail very short. The mouse had adjusted to all conditions of its home—its back was brown because danger often came from above, hawks, owls and foxes, whose eyes looking down into the tangle of grasses saw only a kaleidoscope of soft muted colors; the tail short, for a long one would make it easier to be caught. Perhaps the long-tailed ones did not survive to reproduce their kind.

The red-back, in its way, was as successful as the wolf,

and may well survive its enemies, for its homeland, scattered all over the north from the wooded regions far into the tundras, is often impenetrable to most of them. Diurnal over most of its range, it seldom hibernates for long, and has carved a special niche for itself in the lower third of the great pyramid it shares. Who knows, when the wolf, the deer, and man are all gone, it may still be around, for all it needs is seed and the stems of grasses and the shelter they provide. I placed my quivering captive back near an old runway, and watched as it scurried swiftly into its ancient cover.

Studying the fluidity and constant change of the entire complex of habitats, I could not help but compare the wilderness to a settled country, which in its own way is the sum total of people, towns, villages, and farms, bound together by roads or trails and lines of communication, just as bogs, ridges, and valleys are interlaced in an ecological web of their own.

I learned of the close correlation between beaver and moose, and the ponds that supplied the proper abode for both, the dependence of the fisher on porcupines, of deer on the browse after fires, of lynx and bobcat on snowshoe hares —dependencies so closely related that years of abundance can be foretold by sunspot cycles and the penetration of cosmic rays on vegetation.

Our studies showed that trout require the high oxygen content of deep, clear-water lakes, and bass the shallow acidic waters filled with plant life, humus and decay; that each fish was the result of adjustment to its particular environment and that in the lakes, sloughs, and streams there were many ecological pyramids built into the great ones encompassing them. All forms, tied together through their common base of living protoplasm, responded to the same fundamental needs of sunshine, climate, and soil, all part of the great family, the mayflower, chickadee, pines, the red-backed mouse, and the wolves.

My delight in the world of nature could never be quite the same again—not that knowledge had changed the capacity for enjoyment, but that instead it had accentuated appreciation by making me aware of facets of interest that until then I had barely glimpsed. This was history of a different kind, the long history of evolving species.

No longer could I look at the wolf only for its beauty and general interest, for now I saw how involved it was with all creatures. So complete and necessary was one form to another and to the plants that supplied their sustenance, any disruption could break the chain of influence. To eliminate a red-backed mouse, a spruce budworm, or a swamp sparrow could shatter the fragile mechanism and even destroy it, so delicate were the balances.

The more I learned of basic ecology, the more impressive the wolf became. In spite of the general belief that it is responsible for the decline of deer and moose, I knew that if their numbers varied, it is due not to predation, but to deep snows, lack of winter food, starvation, and disease, often brought on by man's interference with nature's master plan. Wolves are vital and necessary influents in the wilderness, and if removed can change a situation that has been in the making for centuries. If they are taken from the Quetico-Superior, the land will lose some of its character. It will still be a wilderness, but one with the savor and uniqueness gone. Traveling through such an artificially managed area would be like seeing a cultivated estate with game no longer alert to danger. The ancient biological stability would be destroyed in favor of a tame, man-made substitute.

The year I returned to the University of Illinois for graduate work under Dr. Victor E. Shelford, a world authority on the growing science of ecology, I wrote my master's thesis on the life history and predatory relationships of the timber wolf. With my background and observations in the north, it was only natural to choose such a theme. This was the first study ever made of the timber wolf of the north.

As I think now of the richness that comes from knowing one's environment, I realize that with many there is no sense of continuity or understanding, that the howl of a wolf may be as strange and unfathomable as the mystery of a swamp, forest, or lake in the broad pattern of life in the wilderness. True, those who travel far and fast may have a global point of view of seas and continents with needs of different kinds, but the fact remains we are still creatures of the earth and can never divorce ourselves from its all-pervading influence.

Joys come from simple and natural things, mists over meadows, sunlight on leaves, the path of the moon over water. Even rain and wind and stormy clouds bring joy, just as knowing animals and flowers and where they live. Such things are where you find them, and belong to the aware and alive. They require little scientific knowledge, but bring in their train an ecological perspective, and a way of looking at the world.

It seemed to me after I had absorbed this concept my

roots went down more deeply, like those of a black spruce penetrating the tangled mat over a glacial bog.

At long last, I am beginning to understand what Leopold meant, and though it may be true that "Only a mountain can listen objectively to the howl of a wolf," I feel I can listen with more pleasure and perhaps agree with Einstein when he said:

"I am satisfied with the mystery of the eternity of life and with the awareness and a glimpse of the marvelous structure of the existing world together with the devoted striving to comprehend a portion of it, be it ever so tiny, of the Reason that manifests itself in Nature."

We are the music makers
  And we are the makers of dreams . . .
For each age is a dream that is dying
  Or one that is coming to birth . . .

ARTHUR O'SHAUGHNESSY

CHAPTER IX

THE MAKER
OF DREAMS

*T*HE STUDY OF THE EARTH AND ITS SHAPING
opened up new vistas to me, and when finally I was aware
of the intricate relationships of all forms of life in the area,
my understanding grew to the point where I felt more at
home in the wilderness than ever before. The story of Indians, voyageurs, explorers, and settlers added still more
color and warmth, increased by the personal associations of
guides and woodsmen and the men I cruised with through
the lakes and rivers of the Quetico-Superior.

I found during these years that the discovery of any hitherto unknown facet, or even a new way of looking at things, added enjoyment not only for me, but for those with whom I traveled. I learned their feelings about the wilds, and how hungry they were to explore its physical aspects, and anything about the country that made it more meaningful. Loyalties developed to a way of life that seemed the answer to their needs.

As time went on there was a certain fullness within me, more than mere pleasure or memory, a sort of welling up of powerful emotions that somehow must be used and directed. And so began a groping for a way of satisfying the urge to do something with what I had felt and seen, a medium of expression beyond teaching, not only of students, but of those who had been my companions in the wilderness, some medium, I hoped, that would give life and substance to thoughts and memories, a way of recapturing and sharing again the experiences that were mine. The great sculptor Giacometti once said, in surveying his work and dreams:

"Art is only a means of seeing. It is as though reality was always behind a curtain . . . the great adventure to see each day in the same face something new surge forth."

Had I understood then what he meant, it might have explained many things, but I did not know, for the concept of reality as he used the term was incomprehensible to a mind involved only with the visible world and personal gratification.

Days and nights were filled with unanswered questions and wonderings, with trying to clarify values and give direction to my probing, and I sensed vaguely that perhaps, if I looked deeply enough into the wilderness that had satisfied so many needs, the answers might come. My search was so vital to my peace of mind, it completely engrossed me.

During this time I read avidly, steeped myself in all I could find that even remotely had to do with the north, trying to find the secret, not only how others felt about the wilderness, but some hint that might apply to the quest that was mine. Through many books and diaries, I explored the high country of the Rockies and Sierras, the Gold Rush Trail of '98 in the Yukon and Alaska, the waterways and tundras of the Canadian Shield. It never occurred to me that what I really sought was something beyond these volumes and the adventures they held, an entirely different need, the kind of seeing, perhaps, that Giacometti talked about with an interpretation of the land and an emotional involvement that was more than knowledge or superficial enjoyment.

There was other reading too, Emerson, Rousseau, Walt Whitman, Dostoevski, and minds from the distant past, Plato, Aristotle, Marcus Aurelius, and Euripedes. From them I caught glimmerings of wisdom and a depth of perception, man's relationship to man, to his gods, and to the entire universe. The more I read the more I became aware of the need to find a broader vantage point.

I recall the day when I first read *In Defense of Wilder-*

ness, by Euripedes, and the thrill to know that long ago a man mourned the passing of a scene he loved.

> Will they ever come to me, ever again,
> The long, long dances,
> On through the dark till the dim stars wane?
> Shall I feel the dew on my throat,
> And the stream of wind in my hair:
> Shall our white feet gleam
> in the dim expanses?

One day in late October I was hiking back toward town when something strange happened to me, the first of a series of insights over the years. It was as if the thoughts and questions I had been involved with suddenly fell into focus, and in some unaccountable way had been answered so simply and logically, I wondered why I had not known it long before. I looked forward to these moments, for they not only pointed the way, but gave me courage for the task ahead.

It was a melancholy sort of day, skies leaden, the first snow drifting down, a time of introspection in which my own thoughts should have floated as quietly as the flakes themselves. The ground was frozen, ice in the shallows along the shore of a lake I was skirting, leaves and grasses frothy and brittle on the trail, the surfaces of little pools inlaid with long transparent crystals.

The past summer of guiding had been satisfying; I had met many interesting men and explored the lake country farther than ever before. Work in the college had gone well, and the field trips I loved to take had become more and more meaningful because of new studies and observations. I would have been happy and content had it not been for an ever present uncertainty and incompletion that dogged me constantly, the same old questions and wonderings looming as unfathomable as ever, so unanswerable that particular day they almost blurred the beauty around me.

I stopped to rest. A flock of late bluebills were coasting silently offshore, a tight little cluster of black spots flecked with white against the slate of the water. Fall, with its colored violence, was gone, and it was restful to look at the somberness of the shores, the browns, purples, and mauves of hillsides waiting for the storms of November. The ducks barely moved, seemed to keep their position without effort or plan, but even as I sat there, I thought there must be something more than watching ducks, deer, or wolves on my trips into the bush, surely some reason beyond experience or the accumulation of further knowledge, some aim that would give purpose to what I had seen, learned, and thought about. Somehow I must picture the vision within me in a different way than I had ever tried, express my feelings, and catch the country's moods as well as my own.

But how to do this? To explain what the wilderness meant in all its infinite shades seemed an insurmountable task. Poetry might do it, or music, or the colors of a painting, but words, ordinary words—how could they ever begin to portray the sensations that were mine? As I watched the ducks, it was almost as though I had an intimation of what Archibald MacLeish meant many years later when he said, "Art is a human endeavor and the task of a man is not to discover new worlds, but to discover his own world in terms of human comprehension and beauty."

At that time I did not know MacLeish, but the essence of the same truth came home to me that here, perhaps, was my answer, exactly what I must try to do, discover my particular wilderness world in terms of new understanding, describe and paint it with whatever comprehension was mine.

Suddenly the whole purpose of my roaming was clear to me, the miles of paddling and portaging, the years of listening, watching, and studying. I would capture it all, campsites and vistas down wild waterways, the crashing waves of storms and the roar of rapids, sparkling mornings to the calling of the loons, sunsets and evenings, whitethroats and thrushes making music, nights when the milky way was close enough to touch. I would remember laughter and the good feeling after a long portage, and friendships on the trail.

The little raft of ducks floating out in the open were caught that very instant in a single ray of light, and as the somber brown hills were brushed with it, the glow was around and within me. Then the sun dropped behind a cloud and the hills were dark as before, the ducks black spots against the water.

But for a time, I saw them as they were in the glow, and knew nothing could ever be the same again. Had there been the slightest intimation of the long struggle ahead, the many frustrations, the years of hard work and rigid discipline, I might not have had the courage to even dream. If the answer was writing, then it was a tool and medium I must learn to use. What I did not know was that the way I had in mind would take all the resolve I could muster over a long and difficult time, that the real answer to my question lay at the far end of an open horizon different from the rest.

As I came into the little mining town where I lived, everyone seemed unusually friendly, and the main street with its false fronts gleamed, as the hills had. I stopped for a cup of coffee and the waitress must have noticed my elation.

"What's happened to you?" she said. "Find a gold mine back in them thar hills?"

I laughed. "Yes," I replied, "another bonanza."

"No kidding," she said, bringing me my coffee. "Here, drink this and you'll feel better. You prospectors are all the same."

To go into the travail of my early writing is pointless, for all writers, unless geniuses, have the same experience, years of painstaking effort, the gradual growth of facility through endless practice day after day, the interminable disappointments, and the many false starts. Each writer, however, as he looks back, remembers certain milestones, activities, happenings, or events of significance to him alone, perhaps, but nevertheless of great importance.

One of the first for me was taking notes in the field on what I saw and thought about, descriptions of animals, birds, and the countless things observed on each foray into the wilds; until now I had always relied entirely on memory. This was a new activity, and while at first my scribblings were almost incoherent, in time they became more meaningful; but far more important than the actual wrestling with the mechanics of words and sentences was that the very act of recording made me see things more accurately. The longer I tried to recapture scenes and events, the more I saw. I soon filled many notebooks, stories and articles shaped in my mind, and when I finished something I thought was good, I sent it on to the magazines. The fact that these offerings were all returned did not discourage me. There were times, however, when words and ideas came without effort, and I was conscious of something going on in my mind I had not felt before. Golden moments, because they were rare, it was as though writing generated an energy that tapped new sources of knowledge and awareness.

Another milestone all writers will recognize is the acceptance of a first bit of writing. Whether good or bad, it made little difference; the important thing was that for the first time some editor had looked over my work and decided it was good enough to use. What made this a great event was the long time without any success whatever, a period in which it seemed impossible that such a miracle could ever take place.

I had just returned from a guiding trip and was given a telegram. I tore it open, thinking it was a reservation for another fishing or hunting party, but this proved far more exciting.

"Why not write a Sunday feature on one of your canoe

trips," said the editor of the Milwaukee *Journal*, "telling us how you go about it, how you travel, describing the country and the fishing."

This last jaunt with three young men of my own age had been especially satisfying. An exploring expedition, we had threaded our way along creeks and beaver flowages, following old Indian and trapping routes few had ever seen. A glorious adventure, we climbed hills, crossed great valleys, and portaged across almost impassable swamps and ridges. I began writing at once, poured out all my enthusiasm trying to describe the country and how I felt about it. The title was "Wilderness Canoe Trip," a story full of all the clichés, romantic feelings, and unformed convictions any young man might be expected to come up with. I labored for days, wrote and rewrote, finally dropped my masterpiece in the mail just before a new fishing party arrived.

On my return, the feature was waiting, and I stared with unbelief. There were pictures and a map—the spread covered an entire page, but the greatest impact was seeing my name beneath the title. Never again would it impress me the way it did then. This story belonged to me alone, and that day I walked on air, tried to hide my elation and act as though nothing had happened. As I packed a new outfit, the good feeling in me must have shown through.

"What you so happy about?" asked Frankie. "That's a big outfit you're packin'. Don't kill yourself on them portages."

I laughed but said nothing, and when the group joined me a short time later, we were adventurers heading into the blue.

With this bit of success, I was confident the tide had turned, but years went by with no indication from anyone of the slightest interest. The milestone faded into the distance, but my writing continued, for I seemed driven by an urge that could not accept defeat. I dreamed sometimes of the vision that had come to me long before when there wasn't the slightest question, and wondered if I would ever see my goal as sharply again. Perhaps, I reasoned, the medium I had chosen was wrong, the long struggle merely a postponement of the decision to do something else, but I knew there was no other way, and the course was right. There must be faith and hope. Then the vision came again, as though in answer to my indecision, and the dream was reaffirmed.

This time I had gone duck hunting, my goal the rice beds at the upper end of Low Lake, ten miles north of town. The mallards were still around, and I was sure the stand of rice at the mouth of the Range River would be alive with them. It was Indian summer, a bluebird sort of a day as we call it in the north, warm and sunny, without a breath of wind; the water was sky-blue, the shores a bank of solid gold.

I rested at the end of the sandy and boulder-strewn portage. In one place it had led over a bed of slippery blue clay that sucked at my boots, and once I stumbled and almost fell with the pack and canoe. It was good to drop my load and breathe evenly once more.

Across the narrow bay a log cabin was tucked into a clump of aspen. My friend, the trapper, was laying in a supply of wood for the winter, and the sound of his ax came over the water. After each splitting, he laid the ax aside, stooped, picked up the pieces, and carefully placed them on the pile.

For some reason the scene seemed staged in a sort of godlike leisure removed from the normal frenetic movements of mankind, as though it were part of some long forgotten ancient rhythm reflecting the calm and timeless beauty of that October day.

The ax descended, and a few seconds later came the chuck, as solid and measured as punctuations between intervals of quiet. Again the deliberate action of stooping and placing the chunks of aspen, birch, and spruce on the ever growing rows beside the cabin.

I remembered something I had read, that leisure is a form of silence in which one becomes part of all creation, and that true leisure is companionship with the gods. At that moment the old dream returned, and I knew that someday all would be realized. I would be more than a watcher of scenes, part of a golden, timeless world.

I threw my pack into the canoe and paddled across the bay, waved as I passed the cabin, then pointed the bow toward the rice beds. The mallards were gone that day, not a wing or the sound of one anywhere, and it was too early for the northern bluebills, but the time was a happy one for my great question had been answered once more.

When I returned, I went at the writing with a determination that brooked no thought of failure. This time I felt the elusive phantom would materialize, and as though the fates had stepped in, one of my stories was accepted by a national magazine.

For a year or more I deluged the editor with manuscripts, but with no success, and then tried *Trails of the Northwoods*, the predecessor of *Sports Afield*. I happened to know the editor personally, and am sure because of this he bought several hunting and fishing stories, but none with the interpretive slant I eventually hoped to have. Some, however, about animals and birds, held more of the feeling I wanted to convey.

"Papette" was the story of a husky dog with so much wolf blood in her veins she always answered the call of the pack when the mating urge was upon her.

"Snow Wings" was illustrated by Charles Livingston Bull, one of the best wildlife artists of the time. His picture of a white Arctic owl winging its way over a moonlit valley thrilled me as much as seeing the story in print.

Then came "Buck of Tamarack Swamp," an attempt to capture the essence of the frozen north from deer season on through the winter.

There was tremendous satisfaction when the stories came out, for they had something in them that I wanted to say, some hint of what I was striving to express, but most were far from my major goal. Editors wanted action, and whenever I injected the slightest bit of philosophy or personal conviction, it was usually deleted. At first I accepted the editing with good grace, happy to have them take my stories at any price, but as time went on I began to feel as though I had entered a sort of cul-de-sac from which there was no escape, a grinding out of more and more adventure yarns with nothing in them of my own ideas or knowledge of the country. If this, I admitted ruefully, was what I had gone to the woods to find, I still had far to go. What I did not realize was that the constant honing of my perceptions and writing ability, the continual practice in trying to express myself, was laying the background for eventual acceptance in a field I had not even begun to explore.

There was one exception, an article entitled "Search for the Wild," in which I quoted the statement of Thoreau beginning "We need the tonic of wildness," and a criticism by John Burroughs in which he said, "Thoreau went to nature as an oracle, questioning her as a naturalist and poet and yet there was always a question in his mind . . . a search for something he did not find."

To me this was a challenge, and convinced that the lifetime search of Thoreau had been fruitful and what he sought and found in the woods and fields around Concord, Walden Pond, and the Merrimack River was what we all seek when we go into the bush, I tried to prove that the never ending search for the essence of the wild was the underlying motive of all trips and expeditions.

I had dared speak of my deepest convictions, and for once there were no deletions. The first real encouragement I had ever had, it convinced me there was a field for this kind of writing. But again progress was slow, the milestone forgotten, and the next years no different from those that had gone before.

In trying to explain my feelings about wilderness, the time had not been wasted, for facility improved, and the reading and study never ceased. Occasionally when I did no writing at all, my spirits fell and everything seemed without meaning or purpose. The only cure was to begin again, and I found it made little difference what it happened to be, a story, an article, or even the transcription of field notes; as soon as I started, my spirits soared. So infallible was this reaction and so sound a barometer of my state of mind, I was sure that in spite of other activities or the worthwhileness of anything I wrote, I must keep on.

There were times when I looked at the growing accumulation of writings with dismay, wondering if anything could possibly come from all the effort that had gone into them. Even as I questioned, another milestone was approaching, a more important one than any of those in the past. To try and salvage a small part of this storehouse of events, descriptions of places, reactions, and feelings, I conceived the idea of doing a news column rather than stories or articles for magazines; it would be an outdoor column devoted to the central idea that had dominated my thinking. The more I analyzed what I had done, the clearer it became that this might be the solution, inasmuch as most of my observations inevitably developed into short, interpretive vignettes. I worked up a series of topics such as "Smell of the Morning," "Caribou Creek," and "The Pond," and sent them to the Minneapolis *Star Journal*, where they appeared as Sunday features. Letters came from many readers, and the reaction was always the same; I had put into words how each felt about the out-of-doors.

A Chicago syndicate, on the strength of these, made me an offer to do three columns a week for a number of papers in the Great Lakes area. Following a personal interview and a contract, my mind seethed with ideas and plans and I went home to what seemed a new and exciting era.

All my energies were concentrated now on the preparation of material, and I combed forgotten collections of notes in building a backlog of articles that would keep the venture going for a long time. For a year the column prospered, then one by one the papers began dropping it.

"Not enough action," said the editor. "We want more fishing, hunting, and adventure."

The fledgling column of interpretive vignettes was on its way out, and one day came the long expected letter from the syndicate, and I was back where I began. I looked sadly at the collection of completed columns, and lists of titles for the future, and wondered which way to turn. Maybe after all my dream was an impossible one with no chance of realization.

All was not lost, however, for there were many completed sketches and a good acceptance, in spite of what the editors said. More important, perhaps, was that under pressure to meet weekly deadlines, it was no longer as difficult to recapture scenes or impressions. When the work had gone well, ideas fairly swarmed, and some of the sketches almost wrote themselves. I remembered being so completely absorbed I forgot all else in the joy of actually writing what I wanted to say. While there seemed no hope at that time, I had learned a great deal, and strangely enough my determination was strengthened by the battle to find expression.

A new type of writing began, enlargement of the vignette into more comprehensive essays. With them as a core, there seemed no limit to the possibilities ahead, and I felt that here at last was a field, unlike any writing I had ever done. I forgot the failure of the column and went to work with confidence. One day I wrote:

"I have discovered I am not alone in my listening, that almost everyone is listening for something, that the search for places where the singing may be heard goes on everywhere. It is part of the hunger all of us have for a time when we were closer to nature than we are today. Should we actually hear the singing wilderness, cities and their confusion become places of quiet, speed and turmoil are slowed to the pace of the seasons, and tensions are replaced by calm."

This was what I had always wanted to say, and really believed, the secret that had eluded me so long. Here was the dream. The essays would be brought together in a book, or a series of books, encompassing all I had ever done, thought about, or cherished. Somehow the words would come if I were true, and those who loved the wilderness would remember where they had been. I knew how they felt, had listened to their stories, seen the light in their eyes when they spoke of what they had known.

The following years were crowded with new and challenging activities, including an assignment in Europe with the army and State Department. Upon my return, I resigned my position with Ely Junior College to devote more time to writing and the preservation of wilderness in the Quetico-Superior and elsewhere. While my travels took me all over the continent, somehow the essays grew and matured until there were finally enough for a collection, which I called *The Singing Wilderness*.

One of my happiest days was when the distinguished publishing house of Alfred A. Knopf accepted the manuscript, assigned an editor who felt as I did and who understood what I had tried to say.

The artist, Lee Jaques, an old friend, had promised long before that if I ever wrote a book, he would do the sketches. His beautiful set of black-and-white drawings not only caught the spirit of each essay, but embodied his own powerful gift of portraying the north he loved. With his artistry and Alfred Knopf behind me, nothing could go wrong, and I faced publication with confidence.

Even with this assurance, the publishing date set and the review copies out, I waited with apprehension, well aware of the past and how often editors had shied from my particular approach. There was a good, solid feeling within me, however, for I had done what I had always wanted to do—written as I felt I must.

Then came *Listening Point*, the story of my cabin; *The Lonely Land*, an account of an expedition down the Churchill River in Canada; finally, *Runes of the North*, covering the Quetico-Superior and the entire spectrum of my experience in Canada, the Yukon, and Alaska. I know better now what Giacometti meant when he said any creative activity was a way to reality, seeing something new in the familiar, and the truth so well expressed by MacLeish, that the task of all men is to discover their own world in terms of comprehension and beauty.

Once while traveling between Frankfurt, Germany, and Berlin, a Russian gave me a translation of Kropotkin. Though the war was over, its evidence was all around us, ruined cities, stark concentration camps, and the eyes of hungry impoverished people. There was comfort and stability in Kropotkin, and I searched as I always did for the secret of his great success. Then I found it, and all the horror disappeared and I thought only of what I must do when I returned.

"When the poet," he said, "has found the proper expression for his sense of communion with the cosmos and his fellow men, he becomes capable of inspiring millions."

This had meaning for all who were striving for expression. I might never reach his goal, but when I thought of his "sense of communion with the cosmos" I knew at last my question had been answered, and that this was the goal of my life.

No writer is ever satisfied, but my urge now is to make full use of what I have found and known, to keep blowing upon the coals and ashes of old fires to make them blaze again. This is an open horizon entered long ago, and while headlands, islands, and vistas have shown themselves over the years, as I look ahead there seems to be no end to the mirage of water and sky extending on and on into the distance.

Something will have gone out of us as a people if we ever let the remaining wilderness be destroyed; if we permit the last virgin forests to be turned into comic books and plastic cigarette cases; if we drive the few remaining wild species into zoos or extinction; if we pollute the last clear air and dirty the last clean streams and push our paved roads through the last of the silences.

WALLACE STEGNER

CHAPTER X

BATTLE FOR
A WILDERNESS

*T*O EXPLAIN WHY ANYONE IS A CONSERVA-
tionist and what motivates him to the point where absorption
in the preservation of an environment becomes a personal
philosophy means going back to the very beginning of his
involvement with the natural scene. I believe one of the
basic tenets for anyone really concerned is to have a love for
the land, which comes through a long intimacy with natural

beauty and living things, an association that breeds genuine affection and has an inherent understanding for its infinite and varied ecology.

Nourished by constant appreciation of what is aesthetically and spiritually enriching, this inevitably matures into a recognition of the significance of evolutional development. Only if there is understanding can there be reverence, and only where there is deep emotional feeling is anyone willing to do battle. A Spaniard said long ago, "There is only one cause a man must fight for and that is his home." Conservationists fight not only for their individual homes, but for those of the whole human race, the total surroundings of man, the soil, air, water, and all life with which he shares the earth.

When I first came to the Quetico-Superior, I had not thought about conservation. Like most young men who had not been confronted with desecration of the country or the loss of places of beauty, I had never thought that things would ever change, or that there were threats which might despoil the wilderness. I simply assumed the lakes and rivers of the Superior National Forest and the adjoining Quetico Provincial Park of Canada would always be the same. Were they not established as forest preserves by the governments on both sides of the border? Did this not guarantee their protection?

The pine on the American side had been logged in many areas, then burned and grown back to poplar, birch, and balsam. Some places too inaccessible for loggers to reach, or where old fires had raged long before the coming of prospectors and lumberjacks, there was actually no timber at all. The logging dams at the outlets of such rivers as the Stony and Kawishiwi were still intact when I first saw them, waiting for the spring drives and the river pigs who would never come again. To the guides of almost half a century ago, the country with its new slashings and burnings and remnants of the old untouched terrain was still beautiful, with only one purpose, enjoyment by modern voyageurs.

No logging had been done on the Canadian side, but even to our uncritical eyes, it was startling to see the contrast between the Minnesota shores and the dark timber of Ontario to the north. The iron mines we took as a matter of course. To be sure the land was ravished, but we did not question this any more than the cutting of timber. The important thing was that all roads ended there with nothing but bush beyond.

After World War I and during the early twenties, a great road-building program was announced, one which would open up the lake country and make it accessible to tourists. "A Road to Every Lake" was the slogan, and chambers of commerce from nearby communities trumpeted the hope of making the wilderness the greatest resort region of America. No longer isolated, the Superior National Forest would become a mecca for fishermen, "The Playground of the Nation."

I read the announcements and editorials with unbelief. Could it be true the wilderness was to be destroyed? Would the lakes and rivers have roads to them all, with cottages and summer resorts lining their shores as they did in Wisconsin, central Minnesota, and Michigan? Would the silence of such historic waters as Lac la Croix, Basswood, and Saganaga be shattered by the din of outboard motors?

For the first time I was troubled about what might happen. The logging had not worried any of us as long as the lake country stayed wild; trees could return in time, but not the wilderness of the great pines, once the roads went in. We were not alone in our concern, for the men we guided felt as we did. The older guides took the announcement in stride, knowing it had been that way since the first pioneers moved west from the Atlantic seaboard. Woodsmen, Indians, voyageurs, and mountain men had always fought the advance of civilization, aware it was the end of their way of life; they had no choice but to move north or west, following the frontiers and the old freedoms.

This time things were different, for those who opposed the development plan had values at stake they were willing to fight for. To them this last corner of wilderness, bypassed during the days of western expansion, was more important as it was than as another resort country. They had seen what had happened elsewhere, knew wilderness was becoming rare and that the canoe country was the only one of its kind between the Atlantic and Pacific. And so began the first effort to preserve the primitive character of the region, a battle against the decisions of those who had always looked at the bush as an obstacle to progress. This was an open horizon that molded my thinking regarding the preservation of the Quetico-Superior and other wild places on the continent.

As canoemen, we had no knowledge of how to wage a

battle such as this, but what we lacked in contacts and ability, we made up for with our convictions. We wrote letters to those we had guided, appeared at meetings and hearings, tried to explain what wilderness meant to us, and often found ourselves alone, facing older and more experienced men who believed the road program was the most wonderful thing that could possibly happen.

Help came from an unexpected quarter, a recreational survey of the area by Arthur Carhart of the U.S. Forest Service. I had seen Carhart on Lake Saganaga and knew how he felt, but had no idea what action he would take, or that he would advise the chamber of commerce to abandon the road project and protect the wilderness character of the lake country, stressing it would mean more to the local economy in the future.

This was the voice of government, and we redoubled our efforts, talking to any who would listen, letting our friends outside know what was taking place. Locally our pleading fell on deaf ears, for those who heard us could not understand either our point of view or our motives. They still looked at the country from the standpoint of pioneers, and while tolerant at first, when we persisted they branded us as extremists with no comprehension of what was really at stake.

Editorials began to appear with such headings as "Indians or Tourists" and "You Can't Stop Progress." As the attack mounted in intensity, the men to whom we had written talked to editors of magazines and metropolitan papers, and articles came out in our favor.

One summer I guided Will Dilg, president and founder

of a new national conservation group, the Izaak Walton League of America. With him was Don Hough, a former fire ranger with the U.S. Forest Service on the Superior, then editor of *Outdoor America* and writer for the *Saturday Evening Post* and other national magazines. We cruised along the border and inland through the heart of the forest. The more they saw, the stronger grew their feeling that the road-building program was wrong.

Sitting around our campfire on Ottertrack Lake, Will Dilg said, "The League must dedicate itself to saving the wilderness, for it belongs to all Americans," a pledge that has been honored for nearly half a century.

The country became more and more aroused as people from other states sprang to the defense. For some strange reason, this battle had color and drama, gripped canoemen and even those who had never paddled or portaged, as they realized the issue was more than a matter of roads—it was a struggle for something everyone cherished, the right to enjoy wild country.

Finally, after seven years of effort, the Forest Service announced its decision. The road program was stopped and the Superior Primitive Area established, encompassing the best of the lake country. There were rumblings, accusations, and threats of reprisal, but the matter was settled and the furor died. We had learned much during this initial skirmish, experience we would need in the years ahead, and found to our surprise that if people felt strongly enough, if they were truly sincere and believed in the rightness of their cause, they would be heard. The wilderness group had won its first victory and had made friends everywhere.

The fight against roads was just the beginning. Even before it was settled, another proposal was made for a gigantic power development along the international border with a series of seven dams and storage reservoirs that would impound some of the lakes as high as eighty feet. Whole river systems were to be flooded, islands, campsites, and beaches submerged, thousands of miles of bays and shorelines changed to a morass of dead trees and unsightly stagnant backwaters. Far more destructive than logging or road building, this project would not only destroy the wilderness, but change it from a beautiful canoe country to a place of ugliness and desecration.

Arthur Hawkes, a newspaperman from Winnipeg and Toronto, sounded the alarm, and together with such young men as Ernest Oberholtzer of Ranier, Minnesota, Fred Winston, Charles Kelly, and Frank Hubachek of Minneapolis, and Paul Riis of Duluth, enlisted Canadian and American support and created an organization known as the Quetico-Superior Council, with a plan of management based on zoning and balanced use that would perpetuate the resources of the area and preserve wilderness on both sides of the border.

The idea took hold and those who had fought the roads joined forces with them. Canadian and American legions, fully aware of the growing threats to the now well-known region, proposed an International Peace Memorial Forest to be dedicated to the veterans of both countries and the unity of purpose that had come out of the great war.

There were trips to the area by congressional committees, hearings in Duluth, St. Paul, and Washington. Again local newspapers carried the torch for development, pointing out what it would mean to the industrial life of the region. The International Joint Commission, which was established to handle boundary disputes, conducted exhaustive surveys, supervised hearings, and kept a record of opinions.

During this period I made a canoe trip from Lac la Croix to Basswood, and at one point near Warriors Hill climbed a high cliff where I could look out over the fleets of rocky islands to the west with their tall pines pointing the way of the winds. Far below were the familiar smooth white rocks of campsites leading down to the water's edge, winding channels I had often explored, and great cliffs with ancient pictographs. Should the plan go through, these would be lost and buried beneath the flood. I looked at the shorelines of the mainland, but all I could see were the tops of dead trees, ghosts of the old forests.

At Curtain Falls, the site of one of the proposed dams, with the thundering cascade below me, I remembered that David Thompson, the explorer, rested here when he saw a flight of passenger pigeons. The falls were well named, for the water lay like a golden shroud over the ledge of rock which held back the flood of Crooked Lake.

That night I stayed on a bare little island below the triple falls where the Basswood River tumbles in. The moon was full and the swirling caldron of currents and foam was a place of magic and mystery, but all I could think of was what would happen should the dam go in, an apron of concrete instead of moonlit surging waters, the great glacial boulder that split the flow above part of its foundation. The mists might rise again, but the music of that hallowed place would be stilled forever, the enchantment gone.

In the morning I started up the river, portaged around the rapids where voyageurs had so often come to grief, sparkling white waters that would die as the river died.

My next camp was another I cherished, a great rock overlooking a broad expanse toward the west. This was often my first stop heading out with a canoe party, and the last when I returned. The islands lay like black silhouettes against the glow of sunset, the dusk was alive with the calling of loons. That night it seemed incredible that anyone would want to transform such a scene into kilowatts and profit, and I knew in my heart nothing was more important than saving it. Man needed beauty more than power, solitude more than dividends. I could hear the muted roar of the upper falls, sometimes clearly, then falling away, until it blended with the breathing of the trees above me. This too would be stilled.

For nine long years the battle went on, years of arguments, surveys, interminable hearings, while the fate of wilderness in the Quetico-Superior hung in the balance. Then in 1934 came the announcement of the International Joint Commission.

"The boundary waters referred to in the Reference and the territory thereto are of matchless scenic beauty and of inestimable value from the recreational and tourist viewpoints. The Commission fully sympathizes with the objects and desires of . . . those who take the position that nothing should mar the beauty of this last great wilderness."

This calm, measured statement by a dignified international commission were golden words to us. So much national attention had been focused on the area that few were aware of another effort carried on at the same time to protect the region of the interior below the border. Even before the decision, bills passed both Congress and the Minnesota legislature prohibiting logging within four hundred feet of the water's edge, and dams that would raise levels above their natural elevations over much of the Superior National Forest.

For the first time in history, the practice of cutting shoreline timber or building logging dams to flood it out was challenged. If scenic and recreational values were important enough to deny power projects along the border, then, argued the lawmakers, such practices should be stopped in contiguous areas.

One of the most significant developments to come from all this was the appointment by President Franklin D. Roosevelt of the Quetico-Superior Committee to work with government agencies and with Canada toward the goal of sound resource use and the protection of wilderness on both sides of the border.

It seemed now, with national recognition of the area's values and the regulations invoked, that surely the country must be safe. During World War II, however, a new threat developed as flyers discovered hundreds of interior lakes that made ideal landing fields for pontoon-equipped planes, with the entire lake country available for fishing trips and airplane resorts. A boom was in the making, a bonanza that could mean more than dams, the development of hydroelectric power, or any other plan of utilization yet devised.

Resorts sprang into being on Basswood, Crooked, and Lac la Croix, even at Curtain Falls, the most beautiful spot of all. Ely became the largest inland seaplane base on the continent, with pilots advertising guaranteed limits for week-end fishing trips. People swarmed there from such cities as Chicago, Minneapolis, Cleveland, Detroit, and St. Louis.

I recall a canoe trip down the Nina Moose River to Agnes Lake just south of the border when seven planes came in and took off while we were crossing it. The sound of motors was never stilled; inaccessible fishing lakes were being depleted, and campsites were littered with oil drums, paper cartons, and other debris. Sick at heart, we watched what was happening. No place was wilderness any more, and though we sought it in the remotest areas, even after days of paddling and portaging, planes shattered the solitude. Was this, we asked ourselves, what we had fought for, this the country we had saved?

After the war, traffic increased, and as a last hope we applied to President Harry S. Truman for help. Because of the long record of federal actions in trying to preserve the Quetico-Superior, he invoked his famous executive order establishing the first airspace reservation in the world for the protection of a wilderness.

There were violations immediately, with many taken before the federal courts, including the U.S. Supreme Court. In each case they ruled that the protection of the wilderness was a governmental purpose and therefore in the public interest. Following the successful court actions, the federal government was obligated to purchase the many private properties within the area concerned, knowing that without complete ownership the wilderness would not be safe. This entailed congressional appropriations and the beginning of a program still not finished. Millions were spent in acquisition, supplemented by donations of individuals and citizens' organizations such as the Izaak Walton League of America.

New threats have recently developed in spite of all the safeguards laid down—vastly increased visitation, the growing use of mechanized travel, plus the pressures for harvesting timber close to major canoe routes and the construction of all-weather haul roads. The scream of chain saws, the roar of trucks and outboard motors along the fringes of the canoe country were a far cry from the wilderness we had known.

Conservationists pled for the elimination of cutting in the northern third of the Superior National Forest known as the Boundary Waters Canoe Area, the establishment of routes free of motors, and once again the battle raged. The opponents of wilderness protection were adamant in their belief that logging should be continued, resorts permitted in the interior, with motor use allowed everywhere. Studies were made, hearings conducted, new plans of management announced to meet the threats. There was progress and the tide of invasion was stemmed, but those who had been concerned with the region for fifty years knew that sooner or later the old issues would emerge as they had in the past.

We had learned that the pioneer attitude in America is still very much alive with its outmoded concept that wilderness must be eliminated in the interest of progress and used for its resource commodities rather than for aesthetic or spiritual considerations. Though there seemed to be a growing awareness of intangible values, many still had no comprehension of their real impact on the minds of men. While people opposed conservation measures, there was always a hard core of individuals who felt otherwise. One lesson that came from the long effort was that wilderness can be preserved only through eternal vigilance, its main hope a development of understanding and appreciation.

We had the satisfaction of knowing that if any of the battles for the Quetico-Superior had been lost, the wilderness would have been destroyed long ago and the endless controversies ended. We also knew that an aftermath of any major issue, with its attendant publicity, was increased public use. This was a hazard that could not be avoided, for without wide public interest and national support there was no justification for keeping any area in its primitive condition. This fact we recognized and accepted, as long as the principles of protection were not violated.

As a result of my involvement with the effort to preserve the Quetico-Superior, I was drawn into conflicts in other parts of the country where wilderness was threatened, issues that had gone on during the time the canoe country was in jeopardy. Because we needed congressional support, we came to know people all over the United States, the problems that faced them and the areas of their concern, and discovered that while the issues were usually identical, the preservation of wilderness was only one facet of a much more comprehensive pattern.

The struggles went on everywhere with the same old

clichés and worn-out headlines, dollars versus scenery, industry versus pure air and water, ugliness versus beauty. The
battles for Indiana Dunes National Lakeshore at the lower
end of Lake Michigan, Point Reyes National Seashore north
of San Francisco, and the Everglades of Florida were typical.
We argued interminably about saving the Redwoods while
the chain saws screamed and the giant trees went down.
We debated whether to dam the Colorado and sacrifice one
of the wonders of the world, the Grand Canyon; if we could
afford to set aside a Cascades National Park in Washington
or a Voyageurs National Park in Minnesota.

During the controversy over Indiana Dunes, I stood on
the old beach. It was sunset, the water opalescent, whitecaps marching in as far as I could see. Toward the west was
the smoky concentration of steel mills and factories of Gary,
Indiana; to the northwest, the twinkling lights and massive
rosy skyline of Chicago's Loop. Thirty years had passed
since I had first studied the dunes as a young ecologist.

The waves crashed at my feet, the roar of the surf all
around me. For ten thousand years the winds had come
out of the north down a five-hundred-mile sweep, building
the great beach and spewing the sand beyond it. To be sure
there was only a third of it left, about ten miles, but still
enough to preserve and treasure.

Again the old questions: Must this last remaining bit of
beauty be sacrificed for more industrial development? Must
open space and wilderness be lost again to smokestacks,
power complexes, and furnaces? The highest use of the Indiana Dunes was a breathing place and refuge for the millions living nearby.

The answer came clearly above the roar of the surf and from the glow over the great city. People needed those living dunes with their gnarled shrubs and trees, the white ghosts of those that had died, dancing grasses tracing their delicate circles on the sand, the vista of marching whitecaps.

A few years ago the Everglades of Florida began drying, the entire river of grass with the waters flowing through it, the hammocks and lagoons, the home of alligator and crocodile, ibis and flamingo. For millennia those waters had trickled through myriads of passageways, flowing south into the broad savannahs of the Glades. Now that the water was diverted through a series of canals and dikes to the greater Miami area to service the growing city, the truck farms, and industries nearby, the famous Glades were dying.

Ecologists sounded the warning and the National Park Service pled for relief, to no avail. Studies were embarked upon, promises made, but little was done. In the meantime alligator holes were going dry, birds moved to other nesting grounds, fish and shrimp left spawning beds along the coast.

The battle cry now was "People or Alligators." Weren't the tourist business of Miami, industry, and a better tax base worth far more than the scenic and spiritual values of the Glades? Chambers of commerce, the Florida Water Authority, the Army Corps of Engineers were arrayed against the forces of preservation, and once more it was a battle against the well-financed lobbies of developers. Some beneficial arrangements were made, and there is hope that enough water can be restored in time to save the Everglades, but the controversy goes on as it no doubt will for years to come, with pressures mounting higher and higher for still further diversions in the interests of the local economy.

It was the same at Point Reyes in California, a beautiful coastal area eighteen miles north of San Francisco's Golden Gate Bridge. This region lay in the path of spreading suburbia and real-estate developments that would soon sweep over and completely engulf it. Then like many other areas it would be gone forever, only a memory to those who had known the coast before the change.

During the effort to establish the Point Reyes National Seashore, I rode over the hill country. It was spring and the breezes were fragrant with wild lilac and lupine. From a high point on Inverness Ridge we could see the blue Pacific, to the east the dark, rolling foothills of the Sierras. At the brink of a high bluff we left our horses, crept to the edge, and looked down to a shingle beach with its surf and a herd of sea lions resting there.

Old Point Reyes had changed little, and as we lay there it was hard to believe that only a few miles away was the great city of San Francisco. Even louder than the roar of the waves below us sounded the old slogans—Payrolls or Tourists, People or Scenery, Taxes or Poverty. I wondered as I had many times in the Quetico-Superior and in other places what the final outcome might be.

The area was finally set aside, but battles still rage over the acquisition of private lands, the claims of thwarted real-estate operators who missed a bonanza. By the turn of the century, with our population doubled, people will be glad for a place near the great city where they can enjoy a scene fast disappearing along the Pacific Coast.

Not long ago I was snowshoeing a few miles from home on the Kawishiwi River in the area Indians knew as the spirit land of "No place between." The river looked as it did the first time I saw it, the bold, glaciated rocks, the spruce-fringed shores, open rapids steaming in the cold. A moose had walked across before we came, its big tracks going straight over to the other side. Deer had followed the safety of the boulder-strewn shores, and three black ravens soared and circled high overhead, watching the open water and where the ice was thin.

We stayed on the river until dusk, saw the sun go down in a blaze of orange and flame in the narrows, then struck off through the woods, retracing our trail back to the Spruce Road. A truck roared by in a swirl of snow and stopped by a brightly lighted drill a short distance away. A deposit of copper-nickel had been discovered some years before, and now was being prospected by several mining companies.

"Fifteen hundred feet," said one of the men, "another five hundred or a thousand and we'll move up the road."

The motor of the drill was running smoothly, its diamond bit grinding deeper and deeper into the black rock far below.

"We'll have her pretty well mapped by spring," said the driller, "and then we'll see. Several outfits working now twenty-four hours a day."

The little swamp creek from which they got their water had a warming shed built over it for the pump. We stopped a moment to warm ourselves.

"When the mine gets going, it will bring in a lot of people," said one of the crew. "The company will spend millions, lots of work for everybody, a shot in the arm to Ely now that the last iron mine is closed."

The motor coughed, almost stopped, and as the man sprang forward to see what was wrong, it caught again and went on as it had for months. I looked at a piece of broken core. Black and crystalline, it sparkled in the light, a volcanic contact zone between a huge batholith of gabbro and the ancient bed rock. We hiked down the road, and at the turn I looked back toward the rig. Rather pretty, I thought, lit up like a Christmas tree with snow swirling through the spruces around it, the mysterious black figures tending the drill.

I thought of the old wilderness of the Kawishiwi—a new railroad, hundreds of trucks and heavy equipment, a crushing plant, a modern mining development. While government restrictions protect surface values and limit mining developments to lands outside the Boundary Waters Canoe Area, only time will determine its impact.

Faintly I heard the sound of the drilling, the smooth purr of the motor. The world needs metals and men need work, but they also must have wilderness and beauty, and in the years to come will need it even more. I thought of the broad, beautiful America we had found and our dream of freedom and opportunity, and wondered.

Could man in his new civilization afford to lose again and again to progress? Did we have the right to deprive future generations of what we have known? What would the future bring?

The drill purred on and on and the lights twinkled brightly against the black of the spruces—the beginning of a new era, a bonanza, perhaps, or a requiem for the Spirit Land of the Chippewa.

The universal essence of things is to reach a point of view from which the whole of being and existing things becomes visible, enabling man to look at the landscape of the universe.

THOMAS AQUINAS

CHAPTER XI

LANDSCAPE OF
THE UNIVERSE

OVER ONE HUNDRED YEARS AGO HENRY
David Thoreau said: "In wildness is the preservation of the
world." The amazing thing is that he made this prophetic
and far-reaching statement at a time when civilization on the
North American continent was largely confined east of the
Mississippi River, the West still comparatively unknown. In
the East there was still much wild country, and the rural
village of Concord where he lived was a quiet community in
a setting of woods and fields. Even so, he saw portents of the
future, and what he saw disturbed him.

The space age of today is a far cry from the elemental world he knew, for we have opened up a veritable Pandora's box of treasures and powers which have changed the pattern of human life. Scientific advance has brought nuclear energy, space exploration, and satellites in orbit; computers solve problems so complex their meanings are beyond us. Medical science is controlling disease. We are exploring the secrets of life, probing ocean depths and the interior of the earth, moving so fast we are stunned by our progress.

The pace of sociological developments is equally swift; almost overnight there are new governments marking the end of colonialism, the United Nations, the Common Market, World Health, the Alliance for Progress—a multiplicity of international complexities and commitments undreamed of a generation ago. The growth of a communications and transport system is wiping out isolation. Communism and neutralism, new ideologies and religious nostrums are taking the place of ancient beliefs. There are problems of race and poverty and cities torn with violence. The world is in the throes of revolution in which the old moralities and integrities are being challenged.

As if this were not enough to compound and confuse, there is a population explosion at an astronomical rate. By the year 2000, the United States may well have 350 to 400 million people, double our present figure, and the world at large may have six billion. There is no end to the pyramiding of numbers and the resultant shrinkage of living space for human use. Soon there will be no more ground for expansion, and humanity grows as fearful and distraught as other creatures when there is no longer room.

Ours is a strange and dramatic age, the great silences replaced by the roar of engines, the cities vibrating with noise and foul with gases and pollution. The smells of woods, fields, and forests are replaced by those of combustion and industry, and our senses are bombarded with impressions man has never known before. Were it not for a racial consciousness steeped in a background that knew nothing of technology, we might make the adjustment more easily, but physiological and psychological adaptations take eons of time. Too close to our past to ignore these ancient ties to the earth, and in spite of comforts and luxuries never known before, we are conscious of tensions and a sense of instability.

When we remember that only a hundred thousand years have elapsed since man's emergence from the primitive, with vague beginnings running back a million years or more, it is not surprising we feel as we do. Man's life was regulated by the seasons, the fears and challenges of the wilderness, and total dependence on natural forces. Only during the last ten thousand years is there any evidence of culture beyond the Stone Age.

Half a century ago the majority of people lived on farms and in rural small communities, and though cities were growing fast, there was little difference in our way of life. Then spurred on by two major world conflicts, we were literally torn from the countryside and hurled into the whirring complexities of the age and its exploding suburbia. We found ourselves cut off from the life we had known, the insecurity of the frontier ended and an exciting millennium at hand.

Even so there was a sense of incompleteness and loss. Though not unique to Americans, it was perhaps more poignant to them because of the suddenness of the transition. Thrilled by our conquests of space, the detonations of jets breaking sound barriers, and the countless other results of our inventive genius, we are beginning to wonder if it is leading to a fuller life.

In the last few decades we have almost succeeded in weaning ourselves from the past, but in spite of our urbanity, we have not been able to sever our spiritual roots, and I believe this to be the cause of our discontent. With growing divorcement from nature, the change is coming more and more swiftly, and we are now embarking on the greatest adventure and possible tragedy of all, exploring the universe while holding in our hands forces which threaten our survival.

Catapulted into such a dynamic and unfamiliar world, we are questioning the objectives and meaning of our lives. We may seem urbane and sophisticated, but we are beset by longings we cannot satisfy and search for quick panaceas to fill the growing void within us. Because of the conditioning that made us what we are, we have a powerful urge somehow to align ourselves with influences dominant for ages, but are still largely unaware that the solution may lie in a return to our old attitudes toward the earth.

Not long ago I flew across the continent from the Atlantic to the Pacific, pictured the land as it was at the time of discovery, beautiful, verdant, untouched. Whales were spouting off Nantucket, the timber stood tall and dark along the coastal flats. There were salmon and shad in rivers running clean and full to the sea. We passed the blue, misty ridges of the Appalachians that pinned the first colonists to their beachhead for over a century. Deer and elk were everywhere then, clouds of wildfowl darkening the sky. We flew across the checkerboard pattern of farms, over the Ohio, and saw only a vast forest of green extending unbroken to the Mississippi. Beyond the great river were endless plains where herds of buffalo once roamed. The rising foothills appeared and the snow-covered peaks of the Rockies, the broad expanses of the painted deserts beyond them, and finally the ramparts of the Sierras, the dark fringe of coastal forests, and the sparkling Pacific, all in a matter of hours.

The pioneers had done well, facing the unknown and conquering a virgin continent in less than four hundred years. To them the wilderness was a threat, a condition with no compromise, a power to be tamed and harnessed for their needs, so they chopped and burned, made clearings for farms and villages, built roads and towns, prospered and multiplied, and spread out toward the West.

This was work for which they were prepared, and the frontier provided deep satisfactions. There was freedom and adventure, and men lived and died with the light of it in their eyes. Though fear and the brutal realities of the unending struggle were ever present, the period of expansion is remembered with a fierce sense of accomplishment and even joy. One has only to sing the songs of those days to know how they felt. What the pioneers did not realize was that in the process of subduing a wilderness, the very conditions which molded their character as a people were being destroyed.

It was a prosperous land I saw that day, and though there is still poverty and unrest, the good things of life seem available for everyone. Even with the tensions of war in many quarters of the globe, there is optimism and hope. Business is expanding and the national income growing to unprecedented heights. Housing and industrial developments are swiftly filling in the blank spaces between towns and cities. With tremendous ingenuity we have manufactured elaborate earth-moving equipment and have turned loose fleets of the gigantic behemoths to build superhighways through mountains, deserts, and forests. We dam our greatest streams and talk of diverting water from the far north to flush the sewers we have made of our rivers and lakes. Huge-wheeled tractor trains now plow across the tundras to the shores of the Arctic Sea. With inexhaustible energy we are not only taming the last remnants of a primitive country, but molding it to satisfy our wants.

As I looked down at the conquered land, remembering my own pioneer and wilderness experience, I thought of what our people had lost, the old freedoms and challenges, the silences and beauty, and wondered how far we would go in its subjection, if our goal of unlimited exploitation of natural resources and the headlong expansion of our urban and industrial complex would destroy every last vestige of the old America, if our zooming population would increase to the point where freedom and choice would be gone forever. Many refuse to believe resources are exhaustible and pioneering a thing of the past; inherently we are still part of the boom days with development of the wilds the natural course of events. Talk of intangible and spiritual values is never as exciting as evidence of an expanding economy.

And now after four hundred years we are faced with an ecologic crisis which threatens our survival. Waters once clean have become sewers, air poisoned with noxious wastes, soil impregnated with harmful chemicals, the surface of the land befouled with garbage and the enormous effluent of civilization. Our cities are full of ugliness and noise, and the demands of the great society are depleting resources to the point where we see their end. Life moves at an ever faster tempo, and the long, slow rhythms of the past are forgotten in the excitement and frenzy of our pace. We believe science has all the answers, that there is nothing we cannot do. Technology seems able to cope with all problems, confident the age of gadgetry and artificial stopgaps will take care of everything.

Man has emerged as a geological force capable of destroying the earth, and though aghast at what he has done, continues his desecration, confident he will somehow escape the penalty. The fact that in the headlong rush for material goods and wealth he used resources without thought of the consequences bothers him not at all. Nor do the predictions of the year 2000 concern him, for all prophets of doom seem as fanatical and unrealistic as the Isaiah who cried out in the wilderness: "Woe unto them who build house to house and lay field to field lest there be no place where man can stand alone."

The ultimate question is what kind of a world do we want, involving man's whole relationship to the earth, what he does to it and how he feels about what he has done. It implies a sense of responsibility when he destroys or befouls his living place, a feeling of having sinned against man's right to enjoy the earth, that he is ethically and morally wrong. Most Americans do not know the real meaning of conservation, think it has only to do with hunting and fishing, roadside beautification, planting trees, and saving places for picnics and camping. Though these are component parts, conservation involves man's attitude in an age where the one ideal seems to be material progress and unlimited utilization of natural resources. Many ignore the fact that preservation of environment is the greatest challenge of our time, and if we fail to meet it in our obsession with a spiraling gross national product, we will lose our cherished freedoms and the richness and beauty our homeland once knew. We need to wonder about the purpose of man and what constitutes the good society. We must face the ecologic crisis aware that man no longer lives with nature as other creatures but has placed himself above and beyond its control.

We must develop a philosophy which considers the great imponderables, the ancient codes of ethics embodying man's sense of oneness and dependence on nature. While technology may redress the wrongs of the past, it is not the answer unless man's spiritual welfare is concerned. We need an ecology of man in harmony with the ecologies of all living things and a recognition of the truth that our search for utopia reflects fundamental human needs.

"It is a moral crisis," says Harold Means. ". . . The justification of our technological arrogance toward nature on the basis of dividends or profits is not just bad economics—it is basically an immoral act. . . . Our contemporary moral crisis goes much deeper than questions of political power and law, of urban riots and slums. It reflects American society's almost utter disregard for the value of nature."

Over the centuries a host of perceptive minds have believed that if man saw his relationship to the earth and the universe, he could become part of the order and reason that governs his existence, the movement of the galaxies as well as the minutest divisions of matter, a faculty we of the twentieth century seem to have lost.

Bertrand Russell affirmed this thought when he said, "It is possible to live in so large a world that the vexations of daily life come to feel trivial and the purposes which stir our deeper emotions take on something of the immensity of our cosmic contemplations. If mankind can acquire this kind of wisdom, our new powers over nature offer a prospect of happiness and well-being such as men have never experienced before."

If we could comprehend this, we could look upon the earth with reverence and act with wisdom instead of cleverness. When Thomas Aquinas said, "The universal essence of things is to reach a point of view from which the whole of being and existing things becomes visible, enabling man to look at the landscape of the universe," he condensed the entire concept into a shining vision.

Pierre Teilhard de Chardin, one of the profoundest minds of the century, said, "As a man awakens to a sense of universal unification, everything glows as if impregnated with the essential flavor of the absolute beyond all ideologies and systems to a different and higher sphere, a new spiritual dimension"—he too pointed the way to modern man.

In contrast to such cosmic understanding, life for man is a fragmentary sort of existence in which he feels as impermanent and transitory as the things he has built. If he might grasp even an intimation of what is actually meant by the cosmic and imponderables, he would know what the wise have been telling us for ages. If he could believe them, there is still hope for beauty in our land and in the minds of men. If the major resources were the imponderables and spiritual values, there should be no question of responsibility. But what are they? What is their nature, and how shall we know them when they come? The truth is, they cannot be defined, described, or measured, only felt—so simple and self-evident they are often unknown. Such intangible values stir the emotions, influence happiness and content, make life worth living, give richness, color, and meaning to all we do. One cannot explain why a painting thrills us, or a symphony, a poem, a friendship, or love of the land, a corner of wilderness, or the words "Thy rocks and rills, thy woods and templed hills," but we know inherently what they mean.

Such things give dignity and purpose to life; they are part of solitude, tranquillity, and silence, the sense of oneness with living things, and the awe with which we look at the world. No one has ever listed them, but each encompasses the others. They speak to us in such immortal lines as "He leadeth me beside the still waters, He restoreth my soul," or "I lift up mine eyes unto the hills, from whence cometh my help," and we intuitively sense their meaning, and share in a response that has its origin in the primal hunger of all men for beauty, peace, and order. This is what the psalmists felt as they looked with joy and wonder at the landscape of the universe.

Of such are the great imponderables, which deal with basic integrities and human needs, with freedom and the flowering of the mind of man. We tend to forget, but must restore them if we are to preserve the world.

The power of wonder and the unknown are intangibles we must cherish if we are to comprehend our problems. In them was the wellspring of our dawning culture, and from it the first significant expressions of man's mind. Without its spur, scientists, artists, and workers in all disciplines of creative endeavor would lose the challenge to probe and explore. An infallible source of inspiration, it is rooted in man's contemplation of his environment. When we create life, find all the secrets of the universe, and progress to other planets, wonder will have been responsible.

If wonder is one of man's great potentials, playing a major role in the progression of his thinking and knowledge, and unspoiled nature a means of invoking it, here is reason enough for preservation. The stature of man has increased because of beauty, harmony, and the challenge of mystery, not through ugliness, warped and twisted psychosis, and divorcement from the natural scene. While wildness may be only one facet of the entire complex, it can never be forgotten in surveying man's relationship to the universe. No one knows what a glimpse of wilderness means, for such treasures belong to values that uplift the hearts of mankind. Not only have they molded us, but if we are wise enough to preserve them, they will be a stabilizing influence in a rapidly changing world. Should the time ever come when we allow our engrossment with comfort and technological progress to erase our longings to the point where we no longer dream of an unspoiled world, then I fear for America.

And so we have come full circle and are faced with an ultimatum we can no longer evade. Unless we stop the spreading blight over the land, purify our air, water, and soil, save some last remnants of naturalness, our future is uncertain. We know what we have done and are concerned, but refuse to listen, believing that through some legerdemain and infinite capacity to build, manipulate, and improvise, we will be extricated from the morass we have created. We are aware of our predicament, and though we give lip service to conservation projects, we cannot keep pace with the ever growing results of our industrial civilization. If this continues and we do nothing to reverse the trend, by the end of the century we will have an ecologic crisis of such dimensions that the world may well become uninhabitable.

The great challenge is to build such a broad base of understanding, one with such depth and clarity, that it cannot be ignored. Only when emphasis is placed on humanitarian values that affect the welfare and happiness of all will the land be safe, and only when we realize that the real dividends lie in the realm of the imponderables will we do what is necessary to restore what has been despoiled and protect what is left.

Americans have a history of never moving unless confronted with a major disaster. We are now faced with one of greater proportions than the world has ever known, and for the first time are becoming concerned. There are hopeful signs in the general alarm over air and water pollution and the willingness to face the expenditure of billions of dollars to bring back cleanness and order to our land, but these are only indications; the population at large still has other things to think about.

There are those who believe we can have our high technology, continue at the same pace, and still preserve our world. I doubt that this will be possible. The only alternative is to reverse our dominant attitude toward the earth and in our use of it recognize that man is part of nature, and that his welfare depends as it always has and always will on living in harmony with it.

If we can develop love and stewardship, we can look forward to the future with hope and confidence. If we look at our land with reverence, our great knowledge could mean an age of happiness and peace. This is our greatest task, for unless we meet our ecologic crisis and solve its problems as thinking men, there will be nothing to plan for, no utopia, no paradise to regain. If we are able to do this, to look at the earth, not as pioneer exploiters, but through enlightened eyes, only then will the full measure of our evolution be realized.

Juan Ramón Jiménez, Nobel Prize Winner for Literature in 1956, in discussing aristocracy, democracy, and the role of environment, said:

"I believe that in order to be aristocratic, all men, all

peoples, all countries have to live united with their natural environment, with nature in general, for in it indeed we encounter daily symbols and signs which we then have to interpret in terms of the complete social life. . . .

"There is no more exquisite form of aristocracy than living out of doors. When a man can live tranquilly out of doors without fear of anyone or anything on earth, or in space, and not because he is a savage but because he is thoroughly civilized, he has arrived through himself at the ultimate, that is to say, the primal, having rid himself of all that is useless and unserviceable. Yes, this return to the primal is the ultimate to which a man can attain while he is alive; it can make him complete, master of himself, absolute friend to others, a poet without needing to write, without an academy."

Man's problem today is more than escape from the world; he must understand the reason for his discontent and know that while his roots may have been severed, they can be nourished again by nature if he is aware of its true meanings. He must believe that the spiritual values which once sustained him are still there in those parts of the world he has not ravished, and that they can return again when the wounds of the land are healed.

When I first read the sage of Walden Pond, it took a long time before I knew what he meant. Only after years of watching what is happening to America did the full impact of his words strike home—that in wildness, and all it entails in the broadest connotation of the term, is the preservation of the world and the human spirit. His magic formula has never varied for me, and the memories I bring back from the out-of-doors are the same as they have always been. These are the eternal values he talked about, spiritual dividends, abiding satisfactions and simple joys often forgotten in the excitements and diversions of a machine age. These are the moments of revelation, these the great imponderables for which we live.

One of the most vital tasks of modern man is to bridge the enormous gap between his old way of life and the new. Though we Americans cherish the frontier and all it represents, though we pride ourselves on our background, there is uncertainty and fear of the future. None of us is naïve enough to want to abandon what technology has brought, or even evade the challenge before us. This too is a frontier, not only of the mind, but of the physical world. We must make the adjustment and bring both ways of life together. If we can span the past and present, look at our land not as pioneer exploiters but as civilized men, only then will the full measure of understanding be realized.

If we can move into an open horizon where we can live in our modern world with the ancient dreams that have always stirred us, then our work will have been done.

Sigurd F. Olson (1899–1982) was one of the greatest environmentalists of the twentieth century. A conservation activist and popular writer, Olson introduced a generation of Americans to the importance of wilderness. He served as president of the Wilderness Society and the National Parks Association, and as a consultant to the federal government on wilderness preservation and ecological problems. He earned many honors, including the highest possible from the Sierra Club, National Wildlife Federation, and Izaak Walton League.

Olson's books include *The Singing Wilderness* (1956), *Listening Point* (1958), *The Lonely Land* (1961), *Runes of the North* (1963), *Open Horizons* (1969), *The Hidden Forest* (1969), *Wilderness Days* (1972), *Reflections from the North Country* (1976), and *Of Time and Place* (1982). His books created a new genre of nature writing that was infused with beauty and respect for our nation's wild places. He was a recipient of the John Burroughs Medal, the highest honor in nature writing, and his books frequently appeared on best-seller lists across the nation.

For most of his life, Olson lived and worked in Ely, Minnesota, gateway to the Quetico-Superior region.